Lectures
On the Theory
of Socialist Planning

J. G. ZIELINSKI

Central School of Planning and Statistics, Warsaw

Lectures
On the Theory
of Socialist Planning

Published for
THE NIGERIAN INSTITUTE OF SOCIAL AND ECONOMIC RESEARCH

IBADAN

OXFORD UNIVERSITY PRESS

1968

Oxford University Press, Ely House, London, W.1

GLASGOW NEW YORK TORONTO MELBOURNE WELLINGTON
BOMBAY CALCUTTA MADRAS KARACHI LAHORE DACCA
CAPE TOWN SALISBURY NAIROBI IBADAN ACCRA
KUALA LUMPUR HONG KONG TOKYO

Oxford House, Iddo Gate, P.M.B. 5095, Ibadan, Nigeria

© Nigerian Institute of Social and Economic Research 1968

*Made and printed in Great Britain by
William Clowes and Sons, Limited, London and Beccles*

To the memory of
ALEKSY WAKAR
MY TEACHER AND FRIEND

CONTENTS

INTRODUCTION

TABLES

DIAGRAMS

INTRODUCTION

This book grew out of the series of lectures I gave at the Nigerian Institute of Social and Economic Research and at the Department of Economics, University of Ibadan, in 1964–5. In these lectures I tried to present in condensed form some of the results of the study of socialist economy undertaken by a group of Polish economists from the Central School of Planning and Statistics, headed by the late Professor Aleksy Wakar. In addition to Professor Wakar and the author, this group consists also of Dr. R. Bauer (the history of economic calculation in socialist countries), Dr. J. Beksiak (the problems of long-term, perspective planning), Dr. S. Dulski (the theory and practice of economic calculation in Yugoslavia), Dr. S. Gora (the sociological aspects of plan fulfilment, the so-called 'management via social integration'), and Dr. S. Nowacki (the theories of investment criteria). The group itself was formed in 1956 when Professor Wakar became the head of the chair of Political Economy in the Department of Trade at the Central School.

Over a period of years, the partial results of our research were published jointly and/or separately by different members of the group in numerous publications, culminating in a jointly written book *Zarys teorii gospodarki socjalistycznej* (Outline of the Theory of Socialist Economy); Polish Scientific Publishers (PWN), Warsaw, 1965, p. 489.

The lectures presented are directly based on this research and publications as well as on the course 'Political Economy of Socialism' given by the author for a number of years at the Department of Trade of the Central School. Their purpose is to give English-speaking readers a basic outline of our ideas and approach. These ideas are quite controversial ones and cannot be considered as representative of all Polish economic thinking on socialist economy. Rather, they represent one of several schools of thought which can be distinguished in this controversial field.

Having to be selective it is only natural that I have concentrated in my lectures mainly on the problems on which I have been personally working, or which are closest to my interests. As a result, the sociological aspects of management of socialist economy are not touched upon, in spite of the fact that in our total approach we devote considerable attention to them. Furthermore, most of the analysis is confined to the problems of operative planning and the tools of plan fulfilment. The discussion on a method of constructing a perspective plan, which is a summary of two articles by Professor M. Kalecki, is however included as an 'Appendix' for convenience of the readers who may find it difficult to consult the original articles.

My debt to my colleagues is unusually great, as I have freely drawn on the results of our collective research. They cannot, however, be held responsible for the use I have made of this research, nor for any specific formulation these lectures contain.

My special gratitude is due to Dr. H. M. A. Onitiri, Director of N.I.S.E.R., who encouraged me to write up these lectures and was most helpful at all stages of their preparation for print. Mr. J. L. Auspitz not only did his best to improve the English, but also called my attention to a number of formulations which needed clarification. Without his help this book could never have appeared. Anyone who has tried to write in a foreign language will realize how much I owe to his help. If the English still leaves something to be desired, it is entirely my fault.

Finally, I wish to thank for allowing me to reprint or to extract material from my previous publications:

American Economic Review, for an article which I co-authored with Professor A. Wakar entitled 'Socialist Operational Price Systems', March 1963.

Polish Scientific Publishers (PWN), my article 'The Consumption Model and the Means of its Implementation', from *Essays in Honor of Oskar Lange*, Warsaw, 1964.

Economics of Planning, formerly *Øst-Økonomii* (*On Political Economy and Econometrics*), my articles 'An Attempt to Con-

struct a Realistic Theory of Socialist Economy', 'Centralization and Decentralization in Decision-Making', and 'Economic
Tools of Plan Fulfilment' in Vol. 2, No. 2, July 1962, Vol. 3,
No. 3, December 1963 and Vol. 4, No. 3, December 1964,
respectively.

PERSPECTIVE AND OPERATIVE PLANNING*

The process of planned management of the national economy consists of:

(1) the construction of a plan, and
(2) the construction of a mechanism for its implementation.

The essence of plan construction consists of:

gathering information on the state and perspectives of social production,
constructing several feasible plan variants, and
choosing the one which best realizes the goals pursued.

The mechanism of plan fulfilment consists of:

informing the production, marketing and other units of the national economy about their tasks (how these units are informed depends on the type of economic calculation used);
stimulating the units to act in conformity with the plan.

This distinction between plan construction and the mechanism of its implementation is based on different problems that the planners have to solve. The first consists of choosing the optimal set of decisions concerning production and consumption, the second of finding the best methods of putting the decisions into practice.

In turn, the very process of plan construction may be divided into two distinct, but interrelated, processes: in accordance with

* Formulation of this problem is based on several works by Dr. J. Beksiak.

the usage in socialist countries we shall call one *perspective*, the other *operative* planning.

The task of the perspective plan is to work out the desired and feasible developmental path of the economy in the long—or medium—run. Such a projection is necessary for current decisions, which are passed out to production and other units as an operative plan. If we define a plan as a *set of decisions*, feasible and mutually consistent, then only the operative plan is a plan *sensu stricto*, and the perspective plan is only supplementary material, necessary for reaching proper current decisions but not itself a set of decisions.

Usually, both in economic literature and in practice of planning, the *time criterion* is used to distinguish between perspective and operative planning. Short-run plans—for one or two years—are called operative plans, long-run plans—for 10–15 years—are called perspective plans. Frequently, medium-range plans—5 years, for example—are also distinguished.

It seems to us that the time element is a very unsatisfactory criterion for distinguishing between operative and perspective plans. It is first of all, a very arbitrary criterion. (Why a 7-year plan is not perspective but a 10-year plan is, is not supported by any theoretical argument.)

Secondly, we have to realize that both operative and perspective plans consist of decisions or prognoses of both short- and long-run horizons. In a yearly operative plan you can have a decision to start the construction of a new coal mine which will take 10 years to build and then will be operated for the next 50 years, and a decision to switch production of commodity X from one factory to the other, which can be accomplished within 2 or 3 months. And the same is true about perspective plans.

Finally, the time criterion tells us very little about the real differences in economic character between operative and perspective planning.

As a result we propose to distinguish between operative and perspective plans on the basis of the different types of data used in their construction. From this other differences follow concerning:

(1) the time horizon,
(2) the scope, and
(3) methods of plan construction.

Two types of data used in plan construction. In the planning process we use two different kinds of magnitudes:

> *operative magnitudes*, which express concrete tasks addressed to specified units of the national economy; and so-called *statistical magnitudes*, which neither express concrete tasks nor are addressed to any specified unit of the national economy. Their purpose is to picture the desired and probable course of development of the national economy.

We apply this distinction between the two kinds of magnitudes used in the planning process as the main criterion for distinguishing between operative and perspective planning. When statistical data is used, we are in the realm of perspective planning, and the use of operative data characterizes operative planning. Now let us turn to a more detailed discussion of these two kinds of magnitudes.

1. Operative magnitudes are always a result of summing up detailed figures, detailed tasks. So, regardless of how broad the categories or aggregates are in which they appear in the plan, they can always be broken down into their detailed components: *e.g.*, if in the operative plan there is a figure indicating the number of refrigerators per 1,000 population, it is a result of summing up production of refrigerators X in factory A, refrigerators Z in factory B etc. The same figure in the perspective plan cannot be unequivocally disaggregated nor is there any information about the prospective producers of these refrigerators.

2. Operative magnitudes are arrived at as a result of detailed economic calculation in which the whole economic hierarchy participates. Statistical magnitudes are arrived at by statistical methods, which draw into the future the observable trends of development. Statistical magnitudes are not aggregates of detailed figures but are a result of mathematical operations on given informational materials. *E.g.*, consumption of

rayon *per capita* was rising X per cent. in the last 5 years. If we assume that it will be rising $X+Z$ per cent. in the next 5 years, we need a given volume of rayon production.

The perspective plan is not a mechanical extrapolation. It is an extrapolation 'corrected' according to social preferences, subject to all kinds of economic, technical, and social constraints.

3. Operative magnitudes represent concrete planning tasks, which means that they have to be detailed enough to be a basis for action. Statistical magnitudes, on the other hand, can represent different levels of aggregation—different levels of 'generality'. Some of them can be more detailed, some can be more general, more aggregated. A uniform level of 'concreteness' is not required. It can differ depending on information, significance attached to different indices, etc.

Time horizon

We have tried to argue that the time element is a very unsatisfactory criterion for distinguishing between operative and perspective planning. It does not mean, however, that operative and perspective plans do not differ also in this respect. But the differences concerning the time horizon in operative and perspective plans are the result of different kinds of magnitudes used in their construction.

The operative magnitudes always have definite time horizons, which may differ widely, depending on the character of decisions involved. But they must always be specified; this is necessary because every operative magnitude was arrived at as a result of economic calculation, and to carry out economic calculation the time horizon has to be specified. In perspective planning, by contrast, there is no necessarily definite time horizon. The perspective plan indicates only the development trends and there is nothing in the nature of the perspective plan to prevent us from extrapolating development trends for 50 years instead of 15 or 20 years. The reason perspective plans rarely exceed 15 or 20 years is due to the fact that extrapolation for longer periods is usually useless, as too many unknown factors enter the picture. But there is nothing in the nature of the perspective plan which puts a definite time horizon on the magnitudes under consideration.

The scope of operative and perspective plans

An operative plan has to be complete. Because it is a set of interrelated decisions it should not omit any factors or spheres of activity which can affect the decisions under consideration. *E.g.*, the fuel or energy balance of the national economy should include all sources (kinds) of fuel. An operative plan which is incomplete in the above sense is faulty, because the omissions will affect planned decisions in an unpredicted manner—shortages, unplanned surpluses, or substitution processes affecting planned methods of production can develop.

In perspective planning the situation is different. The perspective plan is not a set of decisions but supplementary material for arriving at correct current decisions embodied in operative planning. Because of this, the requirement of completeness is not valid for perspective plans. In perspective plans one can very well have the energy balance for national economy consisting only of the most important sources of energy (*e.g.*, coal and petrol) leaving other sources (*e.g.*, lignite, wood, etc.) unspecified. One can also have a perspective plan which is concerned only with the basic elements of development—*i.e.*, which includes only selected branches of the economy—and omits the rest. The incompleteness of the perspective plan cannot be considered as a sign of faulty planning, which would be true in the case of an operative plan.

Perspective planning can be incomplete, but it must be internally consistent, properly balanced. If there is projection of steel production for 1980, it has to be in accord with the projection of coking coal for this year and all the intermediary years. In perspective planning there may be only a limited number of key branches and/or commodities analysed, but these branches must be properly co-ordinated over time, leaving necessary residua for unspecified consumers or producers.

The development of the theory and practice of perspective planning leads to elaboration of formalized, mathematical models of dynamic balances of the national economy. Several

Polish and Russian works on this subject could be mentioned, but analysing them would be far outside the subject of our present discussion.

The method of constructing perspective and operative plans

The differences between perspective and operative plans already discussed lead to different methods of their construction.

Operative plans are constructed by the whole planning apparatus, from the enterprise through the industrial associations and economic ministries to the Planning Commission. Perspective plans, on the other hand, are mainly the result of work of specialized organs. The nature of perspective plans outlined makes unnecessary the participation of the whole planning hierarchy in their construction.

THE POSTULATIONAL AND 'DESCRIPTIVE' MODELS OF SOCIALIST ECONOMY

The literature on the *functioning* of the socialist economy (operative planning) is the most controversial part of the theory of planned economy. At the level of general, synthetic works on so-called 'economic models' of socialist economy, two types of approaches can be distinguished.

The first concentrates mainly on the construction of *postulational* models, which consider how socialist economy could or should function effectively. The characteristic feature of this approach is the search for an optimal solution, even if it requires making assumptions which cannot be met at present in economic and social reality.

The second approach tries to describe the *existing* economic reality by a theoretical model; not to 'photograph' it, but to reveal its internal logic, its possibilities, and inherent limitations. The characteristic features of this approach are: (1) open refusal to build 'optimal models'—*i.e.*, models assuring the realization of the principle of technical efficiency in the national economy as a whole—because of existing limitations in planning techniques and the availability of information; (2) an effort to understand and explain the *real* functions and role of different economic categories as used in economic policy. These categories (*e.g.*, prices) usually superficially resemble corresponding market categories, but their real functions in existing socialist economies are entirely different; (3) if suggestions are made for making the economy more efficient, there is a conscious effort to keep these proposals within the limits of reality and not to borrow them uncritically from the principles of market-type calculation which will not fit into a different economic and organizational structure.

The common feature of both approaches is their general, synthetic character. The role ascribed to prices, enterprises, consumers etc. can be understood only within the general framework of a given model.

The numerous works on *postulational* models can be divided into two main groups:

(1) market-type models and
(2) econometric models.

An effort to describe them would take us too far away from our main subject, but a few brief remarks may be in order.

Market-type models. The main feature of these models is the introduction of markets or quasi-markets into socialist economy as a mechanism of resource allocation. The most notable example of this approach is still Professor O. Lange's essay 'On the Economic Theory of Socialism'.

A market-type model was advocated by the majority of participants in the Polish discussions on 'a new economic model' (1956–8). For example, the State Economic Council suggested the introduction of independent, profit maximizing enterprises, full cost calculation including interest on capital and rent charges for natural resources and marginal cost pricing.

In this model, the mechanism of plan fulfilment is fully decentralized. The CPB influences the decisions of profit maximizing state enterprises by manipulating so-called 'market parameters'—prices, rate of interest, etc.

Econometric models. The national economy is an interrelated whole: supply, demand, prices, technical coefficients, and production costs are mutually interdependent. Any one of these magnitudes cannot be properly determined without simultaneous determination of others.

Theoretically, all of these magnitudes must be determined together in a system of simultaneous equations. However, the very large number of unknowns as well as our imperfect knowledge of their functional relationships make this practically impossible.

Recently, ambitious attempts have been made to overcome these difficulties. The number of unknowns is diminished by using great aggregates. The linear functional relationship is assumed and electronic computers are used to handle the tremendous computational job involved.

Within econometric models we can distinguish two types with different practical significance. The first are models striving for optimal solution, mainly using the linear programming technique. When applied to partial problems, (*e.g.*, for solving the so-called 'transportation problem') and to many problems within the enterprise and industrial association these models proved very useful. However, when applied to the national economy as a whole, their practical significance is presently negligible, and will remain so in the foreseeable future.

Another class of econometric model consists of the input-output ones. Its objective is the internal consistency of a plan not its optimality. Because of its more modest goal, its practical significance for national economic planning is far greater than the optimizing models. At present, it is already a useful supplementary tool of plan building. But even these models do not presently have operational significance, for reasons we shall discuss in detail later on.

★   ★   ★

Interesting as these approaches are or might be, they have little, or limited, practical significance at this time because of two types of barrier, which we shall call:

(1) the institutional barrier and
(2) the knowledge barrier.

The knowledge barrier applies to both market-type and econometric models. Directing decentralized plan fulfilment through manipulation of market parameters is a very difficult task. Moreover, the price flexibility required for such decentralized management of plan fulfilment is far greater than practical possibilities of price changes in a planned economy. The considerable time lags inherent in management by means of price changes constitute another serious obstacle.

The institutional barrier applies mainly to the market-type model. By an institutional barrier I do not mean that introducing markets in a socialist economy is impossible, but that it is considered undesirable. To limit ourselves to purely economic arguments, it is enough to point out the inherent limitations and deficiencies of the market mechanism in the allocation of investment funds. This is acknowledged even in many Western economic writings. Moreover, it requires drastic changes in existing economic reality with all the difficulties and risks involved.

From our point of view, however, the main limitation of market-type and econometric models is the fact that they are postulational models. They are mainly concerned with how the socialist economy could or should function but do not explain how it does function in reality. It is my conviction that the main task of economics is to explain—in theoretical terms—the functioning of existing economic systems, and not to confine itself, exclusively or mainly, to the construction of purely theoretical models. The attempt to give a theoretical description of existing socialist economies is made in the so-called 'theory of direct economic calculation' (DEC). Presentation of this theory will constitute the main task of our lectures.

DIRECT ECONOMIC CALCULATION (DEC)

Presented in general theoretical terms, the functioning of existing socialist economies reveals itself as a logical and comprehensive entity, having many practical advantages:

(1) it correctly solves, or at least can theoretically solve, two of the three basic economic problems facing every economic system; namely, what to produce in accordance with preferences of the Central Planning Board (CPB) and how to ensure that resource allocation is consistent with the given targets;

(2) it gives the CPB a considerable amount of certainty about the material results, in volume and structure of economic process (reproduction);

(3) finally, in DEC the price and cost calculations can have a very considerable 'margin of error' without substantially disturbing the process of reproduction.

It is no secret that the functioning of existing socialist economies reveals many frictions and shortcomings. To mention just a few, there are:

(1) still persisting elements of the so-called 'sellers' market';

(2) gaps in the real balance equilibrium of the system; the plans are not wholly internally consistent; there are unplanned shortages as well as surpluses;

(3) poor co-ordination among enterprises, as well as uneven levels of operation;

(4) cases of waste of raw materials and means of production in general, etc. etc.

However, we have no doubt that most of the problems still disturbing the every day functioning of socialist economies are not inherent features of DEC and can be remedied within its framework. We may note that this statement is contrary to what many economists, both in the East and West, are inclined to think.

The frictions and deficiencies pointed out can be remedied by improving different elements of DEC. These improvements fall into three categories:

(1) improvements in plan construction (*e.g.*, input–output technique);

(2) improvements in the mechanism of plan fulfilment (*e.g.*, management formulae);

(3) providing what we call general, socio-economic conditions of effective production.

The latter consist of such elements as:

(a) creating a buyers' market;

(b) avoiding economic plans which are too tight; and

(c) creating conditions favourable to social integration, such as generally democratizing political and social life, stimulating social initiative, sponsoring shop democracy, etc.

The inherent limit of DEC is the absence of economic verification of technical coefficients (methods of production). We shall return to this problem at length later on.

The DEC is broadly defined as including both principles of plan construction (known and described as a theory of national economic balance or input-output theory) and a theory of plan fulfilment, a separate problem with its own economic tools.

We call the method of economic calculation used in existing socialist countries 'direct' because in this type of calculation one computes and co-ordinates directly the physical magnitudes. For example, the supply of steel, which is a function of existing capacities and other material and technical conditions, is compared with the demand for steel, which is also the result of certain technical calculations (input norms multiplied by volume of production), when desired final products are defined.

So we see that three basic elements are directly co-ordinated in this type of calculation:

(1) existing material and human resources (capacity to produce),

(2) desired final products, (preferences of the CPB), and

(3) technical coefficients of production.

In DEC we have prices, wages, etc., but they do not play an active, balancing role. In DEC the supply and demand of steel is not, *ceteris paribus*—a result of steel prices; the demand for labour is not a function of the wage level, and prices and wages do not fulfil the equilibrium conditions. There is, as a rule, a direct co-ordination (balancing) of physical quantities without actively using value categories such as prices, wages, rate of interest in determining supply and demand.

This is obvious enough and generally recognized. Unfortunately, the same cannot be said about conclusions generating from it. Nor can it be said about the development of a model of the economic process, in which magnitudes expressed in monetary terms are not used as the basis for economic choice, but rather as a way of representing the inputs and outputs when the aims and methods of production are given.

There are four types of prices used in present day socialist countries:

(a) programming prices, used for the construction of internally consistent plans; these prices are used for aggregation only and prevail in most of the actual planning exercises;

(b) shadow or accounting prices which are used for partial optimization in the process of plan construction; thus far these prices are used in investment and foreign trade effectiveness calculations only;

(c) operational prices used in the process of plan fulfilment, as one of the information carriers used in managing the socialist industry; and

(d) consumer goods prices which are, in principle, market-clearing prices for consumer goods.

If we consider programming and shadow prices together, then we can say that each one of the above functions which prices fulfil takes place in a different sphere of activity (plan building, stimulating state enterprises, selling goods to the consumers). In DEC there is no direct 'automatic' connexion between these spheres. As a result we can have, and really do have in practice, three different price systems. We cannot, of course, exclude *a priori* the possibility of fulfilling all of these three functions by only one or two price systems. Detailed analysis will show, however, that this is not in fact presently possible.

Let us now turn to a discussion of programming prices. The other two price systems will be discussed later.

LECTURE FOUR

PROGRAMMING PRICES

To understand the role and meaning of aggregation and dis-aggregation in planning and the role of programming prices as the main method of aggregation, we have to know more about the *process* of construction of an operative (yearly) plan.

The Process of Plan Construction. As a starting point in our analysis of the planning process* let us take the thesis of the universal character of planning in a socialist economy. By this two things are meant:

(1) There is a universal system of plans consisting of a separate plan for each unit of the national economy. If we assume for the sake of simplicity a tri-level planning hierarchy —CBP, Economic Ministries (industrial associations), and enterprises—there will exist, accordingly, a national economic plan, plans for every branch of the economy and/or industry, and for every enterprise.

(2) The universal character of planning also means universal participation in the planning process. All units of the planning hierarchy take part in plan construction.

Two conclusions can be drawn from what we have said thus far:

(1) Different levels of the planning hierarchy use in their planning process the data with different degrees of aggregation.

---

* The description of the process of plan construction—including diagrams reproduced in the text—is based on a recent article 'System informacji plani-stycznej' (The System of Information for Plan Construction), *Ekonomista* No. 2, 1964, by Dr. J. Pajestka, Director of the Planning Institute of the Planning Commission, Warsaw. We have to stress, however, that Dr. Pajestka does not share the ideas known as the theory of direct economic calculation. On the contrary, he is strongly opposed to them and even uses the quoted article as a refutation of the validity of this approach. To my mind, however, the process of planning, as described by him, is in perfect accord with the theory of DEC, as I am trying to prove in the text.

For example, in the plan of a given coal mine there are many grades of coal specified. In a plan of industrial association these different grades of coal are aggregated into broader categories. In the national economic plan only coal, coking coal and lignite will be specified or they may be integrated into a broader balance of fuel. It is obvious for technical reasons that CPB can make its planning calculations only with large aggregates.

(2) There must exist methods of going from the detailed economic plans of lower economic units to the big aggregates of CPB calculation and vice versa. In other words, there must be methods of interrelating macro-planning and micro-planning. Otherwise, the calculations of the CPB and those of lower economic units will be inconsistent.

This problem of integrating macro- and micro-planning is one of the most difficult in the whole process of plan construction. No one will claim that it is satisfactorily solved in actual planning. But it is essential to understand the existing solution in order to understand planning practices in socialist countries.

This integration of macro- and micro-planning is achieved in practice through collaboration among all planning levels in the process of plan construction.

Before we present this planning procedure, let us put forward two theses:

(1) the higher the planning level the more aggregate data it uses in its planning calculation, and

(2) if the national economic plan is constructed on the basis of aggregated data only, there is no correct, adequate method of disaggregation. In other words, there are presently, at least, no adequate methods of transforming the results of macro-planning into rational (by which we mean feasible and consistent) plans for lower planning units.

The process of constructing the operative plan at the CPB level consists of three steps:

(1) Macro-planning at the central level. On the basis of this calculation so called guidelines for planning are formulated for the lower units.

(2) Aggregation and verification of plans received from the lower units.

(3) Formulation of the final plan and its transmission to the lower units.

This process can be graphically presented as follows:

Diagram 1

STEPS OF PLANNING	LEVELS OF PLANNING		
	CPB	BRANCH OF INDUSTRY	ENTERPRISE
I			
II			
III			

According to Thesis No. 1, the first step of planning is done on big aggregates. According to Thesis No. 2, such a plan cannot be properly disaggregated. In the planning procedure described, such disaggregation does take place but in a very hypothetical way. It is assumed at the outset that the lower units can deviate from the guide-lines they receive, and this is what they in fact do.

In the second step of planning, big aggregates are again used. These aggregates, however, are the result of summing up the detailed plans received from lower units. These plans cannot be simply added up. Such summation will not assure feasibility and consistency of the plan, and could also have results contrary to the preferences of the CPB. So, in the second step of planning, certain changes are introduced by the CPB. These changes, however, are done on big aggregates. According to our Thesis No. 2, such a corrected plan cannot be properly disaggregated. So, theoretically speaking, you would have to repeat the described procedure until the plan achieved by simple aggregation of lower unit plans conformed to the feasibility condition, the consistency condition, and the preferences of the CPB.

If this were the case, the third step of planning would simply consist of transmitting the plan to lower units. Its disaggregation would be purely technical and formal without introducing any changes into the plan itself.

According to formal planning procedure, there is only one round of the planning steps described. In practice, however, these steps are informally repeated through mutual consultation and bargaining about planning tasks. The planning procedure—as it actually takes place—can be graphically presented as follows:

Diagram 2

STEPS OF PLANNING	LEVELS OF PLANNING		
	CPB	BRANCH OF INDUSTRY	ENTERPRISE
I			
II			
III			

Several observations or conclusions can be drawn from what we have said thus far:

(1) The planning procedure just described resembles the iterative process, the process of successive approximation.

(2) Because of technical and computational difficulties, repetitions of the basic planning steps are as a rule partial. All the consequences and inter-relationships of changes introduced in these processes are not taken into account. As a result, the final plan never fully meets the consistency requirement.

(3) Different data and, to a certain extent, different methods are used in the first and second steps of planning procedure.

In the first step:

(a) statistical and similar information is used, characterizing economic potential, development trends etc. of the economy,

(b) the criteria of choice include general economic considerations as well as social and political criteria of the CPB.

In the second step, we have

(a) the aggregation of lower unit plans
(b) co-ordination of these plans for consistency and
(c) introduction of changes into the plans submitted according to the demands of the preferences of the CPB.

(4) Finally, we notice that in non-socialist countries any planning done is usually confined exclusively to the first step described above, the aggregative planning at the centre. The second and third steps are totally absent.

Programming prices as a tool of aggregation. After what we have said about the planning procedure it will be easier to understand the role of programming prices in actual plan construction.

We have pointed out already that in DEC there is a direct co-ordination of physical magnitudes. Because of the limited capacities of planning units in handling large amounts of detailed data—these data are aggregated into bigger groups. The process of aggregation is only a technical tool for planning and the choice of method of aggregation (and disaggregation) must be viewed from a technical standpoint.

There are many feasible methods of aggregation, actually used in planning. One can aggregate according to the similarity of technical coefficients, on the basis of substitution, etc. Even the same goods must be aggregated according to different principles to achieve different purposes and balances. Take coal as an example. When we are constructing an energy balance, calories are the basis of summation of different types of coal. But when we are constructing the transportation balance, the weight is the thing that interests us.

In the process of plan construction, prices are just a tool of aggregation no different in substance from calories, weight or other measures of aggregation. The advantage of prices lies in their universal applicability. One can present the whole economic plan in uniform units and manipulate them freely according to need. Such manipulation makes sense only if one constantly keeps in mind the physical content behind a given monetary value, and the strictly restricted purposes for which it is used.

Are there any special requirements for constructing the system of programming prices?

When prices are merely a tool of aggregation, these requirements are very loose indeed. The method of aggregation is a good one if it properly characterizes a given set. What is 'proper', however, depends on the aim of aggregation. Our example with coal aggregated according to calories or to weight illustrates this. Because there is a need for many methods of aggregation for different purposes, and because almost any set of prices can be used for aggregation, in practice the *operative prices* and consumer goods prices as of a given date, *e.g.*, January 1960 are used in plan construction. Operative and consumer prices change over time but as programming prices they remain constant for at least the whole 5-year period.

These prices are set for different purposes and on different principles. *E.g.*, some operative prices are fixed on a cost-plus basis, some on the basis of substitution principle etc. Consumer goods prices—as we shall see in detail later on—are usually fixed at the level which clears the market. This diversity, however, does not preclude their use as programming prices.

Our discussion up to this point has been based on a tacit assumption that the aggregation and programming are confined to individual branches of the economy or to individual balances. But what about the balance for the national economy as a whole? Would the existing programming prices do the job?

Obviously not. For this, a uniform system of programming prices is required. But we are describing actual practice, where we do not construct the overall economic balance for the national economy. The planning organs use many different balances, covering different branches or aspects of the national economy and these balances are constructed on the basis of different monetary and physical units. This does not, however, preclude the possibility of achieving an equilibrium of the plan. The co-ordination and balancing is done in practice through the iterative process of planning procedure already described. Needless to say, perfect balancing cannot be achieved by such a process. The only practical answer to this problem is to devise plans which are not over strained and thus allow for proper reserves. This is the best we can do until the input-output tables have operational value.

At present, however, we do not construct *ex ante*, but only *ex post facto* input-output tables, which are much too aggregative to serve as an operational plan. Let us discuss this problem in more detail.

Input-output analysis and operative planning. We have said that existing planning procedure does not allow us to construct a fully balanced plan. If this is the case why do we not use the input-output technique, which theoretically enables us to achieve both general and partial equilibrium of the plan?*

Before 1960 only 49 statistical input-output tables were constructed in the whole world. They were made for twenty-seven countries and their magnitudes are shown in the following table.

Table 1

	Number of input-output tables with:					
	less than 30 rows	between 30–50 rows	between 50–100 rows	between 100–150 rows	above 150 rows	Total
Total	19	14	7	6	3	49
In socialist countries	1	3	2	1	—	7

Thus far input-output tables are not a method of plan construction. They are mainly calculated *ex-post* to help us

* The following remarks are based on Dr. K. Porwitt's article 'Zastosowanie metody nakladow-wynikow w praktyce planowania i analiz ekonomicznych' ('The Application of Input-output Method in Practice of Planning and Economic Analysis'), *Ekonomista* No. 6, 1963.

better understand inter-relationships in national economy and the consequences of certain changes in planned goals or methods of production. (*E.g.*, in Poland, the Central Statistical Office finished in 1964 the input-output table for 1962, 140 × 140.) At present, input-output tables only indirectly improve operative planning. A brief review of some difficulties in constructing input-output tables will explain why they are not as yet directly applied to such planning.

First of all, we do not have sufficient statistical and planning information to construct a full, comprehensive input-output table. Moreover, collecting additional information is a long and expensive process which requires complete reorganisation of national statistics. We have to remember that in all countries the statistical requirements were formulated *before* possibilities of using input-output technique were recognized. Presently, data making up the plans of economic ministries and industrial associations are insufficient for constructing input-output tables and are in a form unsuited to such calculations.

Secondly, we have to remember that construction of an input-output table requires the satisfactory solution of certain statistical and conceptual problems. Let me mention only one, but of a fundamental nature.

The principles of so-called 'perfect aggregation' require that commodities be aggregated on the basis of identical input structure, necessary for their production. Only when this requirement is fulfilled can the calculation on big aggregates be later translated into operational decisions. However, adherence, to the 'perfect aggregation' principle requires a very big input-output table. Even several hundred rows would not be enough. Classification of branches of production based on aggregation of data for whole enterprises, which are generally multi-product and moreover have different technical coefficients for the same product, cannot be considered correct. This, however, is the existing practice.

Let us assume that the Planners have a statistical input-output table for a given year at their disposal. For example, the Polish Planning Commission had in 1964 an input-output table (140 × 140) for 1962. What are the practical consequences of this? To what extent will it facilitate and improve the process of operative planning?

On the basis of the input-output table we can make a comparative analysis of several plan variants, tracing different consequences (*e.g.*, impact on balance of payments) of changes in desired final products, in methods of production, etc. In carrying out this analysis, however, we have to remember that:

(1) We are using statistical (historical) technical coefficients, when the actual level of technical coefficient is constantly changing due to changing methods of production of individual commodities and changes in the internal structure of individual branches of industry. To remedy this, one can use 'planned technical coefficients' which is the usual practice, but, obviously enough, these coefficients represent only approximations and thus contain a substantial margin of error.

(2) Secondly, we have to remember that our calculations whether based on statistical or planned technical coefficients are not tantamount to constructing the operative plan. All input-output calculations deal with magnitudes (output, input, consumption, investment etc.) aggregated according to their material content, whereas in constructing the operative plan we have to take into account classification according to organizational units. There would be no complications if technical coefficients were the same irrespective of the producer of a given output. This, however, is not the case. Technical coefficients differ widely between different organizational units. Recalculation of the conventional input-output table to get a table accounting for this fact is practically impossible, because it requires an input-output table of a magnitude far exceeding our present possibilities.

As a result, until the input-output technique has operational value, we have to use the planning procedure described. It is far from ideal, but it is thus far the only practical method. At the same time, no effort should be spared to increase the practical significance of input-output analysis.

THE EXTERNAL CHARACTER
OF METHODS OF PRODUCTION

In the general description of DEC with which we began our analysis of operative planning, we pointed out that the inherent limit of DEC is the lack of economic verification of technical coefficients (methods of production). Now it is time to discuss this problem in detail.

By economic verification we mean meeting the requirements of the principle of technical efficiency. The economic system is efficient when any further increase of final goods can be achieved only by diminishing production of another final good. [1] In other words:

> 'When production is so organized that society cannot get more of any one output without sacrificing other outputs or expending additional inputs, and cannot use less of any one input without using more of other inputs, or sacrificing outputs, we can say that it is organized optimally.'[2]

This is, of course, a technical optimum, which is achieved when the ratio of physical marginal productivities of means of production is equalized in all uses, or when, subject to the fulfilment of certain other conditions, $MC = P$ in the whole national economy.

The essence of our thesis about the external character of methods of production in DEC can be summarized as follows:

The method of economic calculation used in DEC does not allow us to meet the requirements of technical efficiency.

The character of economic calculation applied in DEC does not allow us to say with certainty if the changes involving substitutability which are introduced in production methods put us nearer to or further from the technically efficient solution.

The essence of plan construction in DEC consists of (1) formulating the final goods desired, (2) multiplying them by a matrix of technical coefficients, (3) determining the gross outputs needed, and (4) adjusting both goals and methods of production so that the plan is feasible and consistent.

It is easy to see that we are within the framework of input-output analysis. The fact that this is done not through formal input-output calculation but through the planning procedure described, does not change the inherent limitations of this approach.

Its 'fundamental assumption'—if I may use Professor W. Leontief's expression—is that the quantity of each kind of input absorbed per unit of given output is technologically determined and thus can be treated as a structural constant. 'In treating technical input coefficients as independent structural parameters, this approach assumes them to be independent of the prices of the respective cost factors and thus eliminates from this particular general equilibrium model the "substitution effect" of the marginal productivity theory. This can be considered to be its fundamental weakness.' [3]

The meaning of what we have said thus far is that the methods of production used in DEC are external to the system. They are not verified within the system but are taken from outside it and constitute its unverified data. They may be the so-called 'traditional' methods of production, by which we mean statistical technical coefficients, or the so-called 'advanced' methods of production which are statistical technical coefficients that have been corrected on the basis of the envisaged investment plan, the practice of more advanced countries, and existing technical know-how before being used as data for plan building by the country under consideration.

The consequences of this are far-reaching. The external character of the methods of production means that:

(1) plans can satisfy only consistency conditions but not optimality conditions;

(2) the planning process and the planning tools required for it are greatly simplified. In this situation the main objective of operative planning is to achieve a balance between output and capacities in aggregates and internal consistency among the sectors;

(3) the character, role and functions of prices in operative planning are determined.

We have repeatedly said that the choice of optimum techniques is not possible in DEC. It cannot be calculated in advance and there is no subsequent mechanism which will indicate what changes in chosen methods of production would be advisable from the viewpoint of technical optimum. In such a situation, the best we can do is to create the mechanism which will assure the closest possible realization of the *chosen* methods of production, as this will at least assure us of a 'balanced equilibrium' and the avoidance of shortages and bottlenecks. The operational prices have an important role to play here.

The external character of the methods of production should not imply that they can be random and that economic analysis plays no important role in their choice. Proper economic analysis of the methods of production is an absolutely necessary goal but it is also a far less ambitious one than the realization of technical efficiency in the national economy as a whole. The purpose of economic analysis in the choice of method of production in DEC is to choose such technical coefficients as will assure the desired level of employment and—in the light of the desired final products and resources available—will take into account, as fully as possible, the constraints existing in the system.

Some further comments are necessary here.

We have said that the main tasks of the operative plan are to achieve a given level of employment, and given final products, which in turn broadly determine the structure of employment.

If the existing technical coefficients were treated as given and constant, the only way of achieving a feasible and consistent plan would be to introduce the necessary changes in the volume and structure of planned tasks.

But this is obviously not the case. Before we change the planned goals, we try to manipulate the technical coefficient to maximize the planned goals.

For example, in discussing the Polish perspective plan for 1960–75, Professor Michal Kalecki pointed out that in our planning practice we do not assume constant technical co-efficients. Parts of the changes in technical coefficients have, let us say, an 'automatic' character. For instance, a substantial increase in new power plants automatically leads to a decline in the amount of coal per 1 kwh of electric energy. Another, and probably more important, type of change in technical coefficients results from conscious choices of methods of pro-duction, choices which aim at securing the balanced equilibrium of the plan with minimum changes in desired structure of final products. For example, the electrification of railroads diminishes the demand for coal, the development of chemical industry diminishes the demand for natural fibres, wood, steel etc. [4]

The problem of manipulating the methods of production for the sake of achieving equilibrium in the plan was again one of the most crucial in the discussion of the current Polish 5-year plan, 1966–70. The demographic situation (the fact that the active labour force will increase 10 per cent. in these years) requires the labour-intensive type of development and maxi-mum economy in the use of the investment fund. These can be achieved by appropriate changes in the *structure* of production or *methods* of production or through a combination of both. In his recent article [5], Professor Kalecki warned against relying too strongly on changes in the *structure* of production instead of in *methods* of production. The former can easily turn out to be unrealistic. There are relatively narrow limits in changing the structure of export and of home demand, moreover undesir-able changes in the structure of consumption can result. Hence Professor Kalecki advocates more active manipulation of methods of production in order to equilibrate the plan without profound changes in the desired final products.

The process of plan construction can then be depicted as a process of successive approximation during which we seek how best to achieve the planned goals by appropriate changes in methods of production. Let us describe this process in more detail:

> We start with given production and employment tasks.
>
> Taking these as a first guide-line, we assume a certain matrix of technical coefficients.
>
> By multiplying it, we achieve the necessary gross output. By comparing the necessary gross output with existing capacities (and their planned increase), we get the set of shortages and surpluses.
>
> We take these shortages and surpluses as a starting point in looking for appropriate changes in technical co-efficients which would enable us to overcome these barriers.
>
> At a certain point in this process we have to give up and introduce necessary changes in planned goals. These changes are as a rule less far-reaching than what would have been needed if the originally assumed matrix of technical coefficients had been accepted at the outset without any effort to introduce changes into methods of production.

The shortages and surpluses which in our model play the role of guide-lines for changing technical coefficients need some further explanation. These shortages and surpluses result from existing capacities, desired final products, and technical coefficients assumed in the first trial.

The third element is especially important. It is intuitively obvious that different assumed technical coefficients will produce different sets of shortages and surpluses. If the process of changing the technical coefficients were continued until the technical efficiency of production were achieved, the initial set of technical coefficients would have no impact on the final plan. It could only prolong or shorten the necessary calculations. If, however, as is the case in practice, this process of successive changes in technical coefficients has to stop after a few rounds, and, more important, the rules of the game do not allow us to aim at technical efficiency, the starting point influences the volume and structure of a final plan.

In contrast to the model which verifies the methods of production, where the starting point does not influence the final result (*e.g.*, in the Lange model we can take as a starting point of his 'trial and error method' both historical prices and incidental prices), in the DEC model the starting point in choosing methods of production does influence the finally accepted methods of production and the volume and structure of the final plan.

The partial verification of methods of production in DEC. In discussing the problem of choice of production techniques in DEC we have to discuss separately the possibilities of partial verification of methods of production with the help of operations research.

We are talking here about *verification* of methods of production and not just about their choice because these techniques aid us in achieving the technical efficiency of production.

We speak of *partial* verification, not only because these techniques exclude or ought to exclude the processes of substitution, but also because they are limited to individual enterprises or branches of the economy.

Even if these techniques were used in all enterprises it would not be tantamount to achieving technical efficiency of production, because we exclude substitution processes, and the sum of partial optimal solutions does not necessarily lead to general optimum.

As examples of the use of the operations research for partial verification of methods of production we can mention: solving the so-called 'transportation problem' with the help of linear programming, or attaining plan fulfilment of a branch, enterprise or its division with less of a given input without increasing other inputs, or overfulfilling planned tasks without increasing any inputs.

Summing up what we have said thus far, even the best possible manipulation of technical coefficients to maximize the planned tasks does not lead at present to economic verification of methods or production. All the steps which can be and are undertaken are examples of partial analysis which, by its very nature, does not lead to technical efficiency of production.

At the same time, what we have said indicates the importance of conscious manipulation of the methods of production both for achieving the planned goals and for overcoming the many barriers the planners encounter in their efforts to construct the feasible and consistent plan.

The choice of optimal technology in a market economy. We have said repeatedly that the choice of optimal technology—technology delivering the maximum possible volume of goods with given resource availability—is not possible within the framework of DEC, at least at present. But is such a choice of optimal technology possible in a market economy which tries to construct an investment plan ? I do not think so for two reasons:

(1) It is generally recognized that in the developing countries existing prices of means of production are not equilibrium prices. The capital is undervalued, the labour overvalued, and the level of these distortions is usually quite substantial. In a recent UN publication the authors say, for example that in many underdeveloped countries '. . . an accounting wage of 50 per cent. of market wages and an accounting interest rate of 200 per cent. of market rates for commercial loans may reflect the relative scarcities of capital and labour more accurately than the market prices themselves'. [6]

But this is not all. The market prices—in any market economy, developed as well as underdeveloped—also differ as a rule from the social value, because the former do not reflect external economies in production, external benefits in consumption and other factors which have to be taken into account in the choice of optimal technique.

(2) It is generally recognized that the choice of optimal technique cannot be solved satisfactorily by any partial analysis. One cannot choose a technique for one commodity irrespective of that for the others, so the problem can be solved only in terms of a set of simultaneous equations. Needless to say, the knowledge barrier for this is not less but more acute in any market economy than in the socialist economies.

Summing it up, I think that when we take into account the existing level of market imperfections, the inherent divergence between market prices and social values and the inadequacy of any partial analysis, we have to admit that the choice of optimum technology, from the point of view of the National Economy as a whole, and not from the point of view of the income accruing to the private investor alone, is impossible not only in DEC but in any market economy, underdeveloped as well as developed. At the same time socialism provides full employment of resources, higher level of investment, and an approach to the problem of investment decisions, which derives explicitly from the general equilibrium point of view. By contrast, most investment decisions in the market economy are undertaken (or not undertaken) only too often on the basis of individual profitability alone.

In other words, neither the market economy, nor the socialist economy have at their disposal a system of real scarcity prices. The best admission of this obvious but rarely mentioned fact is the work going on in both the East and West to construct a comprehensive system of 'true parameters'. As examples, we can point out so-called 'objectively determined valuations' of Professor Kantorowicz [7] or 'accounting prices' of Qayum. [8]

Forty years ago Professor L. von Mises said that only the market can supply proper data for economic calculation. From this far-reaching conclusions were drawn, concerning among others 'the inherent irrationality' of decisions in non-market socialist economy. Presently, almost all Western economists admit that the market does not provide, from the standpoint of technical efficiency, the correct data for constructing the national economic plan. Qayum's book quoted above is exactly an effort to construct a system of parameters differing from the market ones to be used by Planning Organs to properly steer the national economy. The very assumption of this book is the fact that market parameters cannot be such a guide if an efficient solution is desired. With this admission, which presently is rather general, a certain stage in the history of economic thought is already behind us.

REFERENCES

[1] See T. C. Koopmans, *Uses of Prices*, Cowles Commission Papers. Special Paper No. 3, Chicago 1959, p. 3.

[2] J. de Graaff, *Theoretical Welfare Economics*, Cambridge University Press, 1957, p. 14.

[3] W. Leontief, Econometrics in 'A Survey of Contemporary Economics', R. D. Irwin, 1952, Vol. 1, p. 409.

[4] See M. Kalecki, *Plan perspeektywiczny na lata* 1961/75 (*The Perspective Plan for 1961/75*), Nowe Drogi, August 1958, pp. 43-4.

[5] M. Kalecki, *Uwagi o planie gospodarczym na lata 1966/1970* (*Remarks on the Economic Plan for 1966–70*), Zycie Gospodarcze, No. 15/1964.

[6] *Programming Techniques for Economic Development*, Bangkok, 1960, p. 42.

[7] L. V. Kantorowicz, *Ekonomicheskii raschet nailuchshego ispolzovaniia resursov* (*Economic Calculation of the Best Use of Resources*), Moscow, 1959.

[8] P. Qayum, *Theory and Policy of Accounting Prices*, Amsterdam, 1960.

THE INDICES OF INVESTMENT EFFECTIVENESS IN DIRECT ECONOMIC CALCULATION

After what we have said about the choice of methods of production in DEC, a question inevitably springs to mind. What are the role and character of the indices of investment effectiveness in a planned economy? These indices occupy a very prominent place in discussions of planned economy in both Eastern and Western economic writings.

Before we discuss the merits and demerits of the indices of investment effectiveness actually used in planning practice, let us say a few words about them in general.

As we have said, the CPB is looking for such methods of production as will maximize desired final products of a given physical and time structure and assure a given level of employment.

At the same time, it is not the CPB which 'elaborates' methods of production. This is done by hundreds of specialized 'project bureaux'. And here we come to the functions of indices of investment effectiveness in DEC.

The main task of indices of investment effectiveness is to pass to the project bureaux the requirements of the CPB concerning the desired methods of production at a given stage of economic development. *E.g.*, such requirements as less use of means of production imported from the Common Market countries, substitution of wood by plastics, etc.

Together with these specific requirements reflecting the existing or more often, the anticipated situation in the equilibrium of the plan, the CPB is always interested in efficient use of capital, maximization of product per unit of capital and per unit of time because investment funds are always limited in relation to demand.

Investment coefficients, then, simultaneously ought to transmit these two requirements to the project bureaux:

(1) efficient use of capital, *i.e.*, preparing economical investment projects, and

(2) consideration of the anticipated 'balance scarcity' of given means of production.

Theoretically, they can be achieved by introducing the price for the use of capital, by charging an interest rate in some form, and by creating a price policy for means of production which will reflect their future balance scarcities and hence their anticipated prices when the construction and/or production begin.

Meeting the first requirement is not too difficult in DEC. In DEC the price of capital is a tool for equilibrating the supply and demand for capital; it is the additional requirement which methods of production have to meet. The main task of the price of capital in DEC is to counter-balance a tendency likely to occur in project bureaux of elaborating the technically best methods of production without due regard to scarcity of capital and the employment goals of the plan. The rate of interest that will provide this counter-balance can only be found by trial and error.

Meeting the second requirement entails the introduction of coefficients to correct existing operative prices. To explain this we have to anticipate our future discussion of operative prices and say a few words about them now.

The only full system of prices which the CPB has at its disposal is the system of operative prices. These prices are used from a given date for the purpose of plan construction as so-called programming prices. Unfortunately, however, neither set of prices is suitable for guiding the project bureaux' programming prices for very obvious reasons. Prices for project bureaux are not used for aggregation, but to communicate future or existing scarcities. The programming prices *ex definitione* cannot do this job.

If we turn to operative prices, the problem is more complicated. Leaving fuller discussion for later, we can say that in practice operative prices also do not reflect existing 'planned scarcities' correctly, but even if they did, they could at most reflect the current market situation. They do not and cannot reflect *future* scarcities, a necessity for proper guidance of project bureaux.

It would be inefficient and uneconomical to ask project bureaux to anticipate future prices, as the capitalist investor must. Moreover, the CPB influences them to a great extent through its investment and foreign trade policies.

As a result the CPB should inform the project bureaux about future scarcities by supplying them with time series of future prices. In practice, this can be done and sometimes is done, by supplying the project bureaux with corrective coefficients to the existing system of operative prices. *E.g.*, in calculating the investment effectiveness, accounting rather than current prices for imports are used.

Through such a policy the CPB can get from project bureaux the methods of production most closely conforming to expected future scarcities. This seems to us the most one can achieve in investment calculation within the framework of DEC. For choosing between projects within a given branch of the economy, many methods can be used, some of which we shall discuss in the next section. However, irrespective of the actual method of choosing between projects, the two requirements explained thus far have to be met to make this choice sensible and economically valid in the limited sense already explained.

*The formulae of investment effectiveness.** Before we can proceed to a critical examination of the indices of investment effectiveness actually used in Polish investment planning, we must again stress their limited role. Professor Kalecki has expressed it with admirable clarity:

* In what follows I am especially in debt to Professor A. Wakar's article '*Wskazniki efektywnosci ekonomicznej inwestycji*' (*Indices of Economic Effectiveness of Investment*), Economista No. 1, 1957, and to Dr. S. Nowacki's article 'Kierunki dyskusji o efektywnosci inwestycji w gospodarce socjalistycznej' (*Trends in the Discussion on Investment Effectiveness in Socialist Economy*), Zeszyty Naukowe SGPS Nr. XVIII.

'. . . in the course of ascertaining the demand for products of a single industry generated by the home components of national income, the problem of choosing between various technological alternatives will be encountered. For example, the choice between electrification and dieselization of railways as being dependent upon the traffic load of a given line may be quoted. In order to settle such problems, it is necessary to have a *method* for comparing the efficiency of two technological alternatives producing *the same final effects* [my italics—JGZ]. Such methods have in fact been developed in Poland as well as in other socialist countries.

'A similar problem arises in connection with various possibilities of earning foreign exchange by means of exports or substituting home production for imports. In order to compare alternative ways of earning one dollar in foreign trade, one can apply the same method used to compare technological alternatives for achieving the same final productive effect. . . .

'It should be added that for these purposes, the calculation of efficiency should be applied as thoroughly as possible, and such is the case in Poland and other socialist countries. On the other hand, *there is no point in applying them for anything other than the choice of technological alternatives or the examination of the structure of foreign trade* [my italics JGZ].'

'Apart from these two aspects, the structure of output in a planned economy cannot be determined by considerations of efficiency. Indeed, in an economy which would be closed and where only one method of achieving a given final productive effect were available, the calculations of efficiency would be out of place. For, as follows from the above argument, with a given growth rate of the national income, a given relation between unproductive investment and consumption, and a given structure of consumption, the industrial structure of output would be fully determined by the technical coefficients of production.' [1]

Bearing this in mind, we can turn to the 'method for comparing the efficiency of two technological alternatives producing the same final effect' used in Poland's investment planning. The main criticisms of this method can be conveniently divided into two parts:

(1) the very formula used for calculating efficiency of investment may be deficient, and

(2) the parameters used in the formula may be deficient.

The first 'synthetic', overall formula for calculating the effectiveness of investment was issued by the Polish Planning

Commission in February and August (revised version) of 1956. This formula had the following form:

$$E = \frac{I + Iqn + K}{P}$$

where:

I = investment outlays

K = prime costs and maintenance costs for the whole period of use-life of investment

q = so-called 'coefficient of profitability'

n = period of use-life of investment, and

P = amount of production in 'n' years in physical terms.

A numerical example will clarify the functioning of this formula. Let us analyse two 'technological alternatives' A and B, assuming $q = 0 \cdot 1$

	Investments	
	A	B
I	$310	$200
K	$ 90	$200
P	12 pieces	10
n	10 years	5

If we use the above data in our formula, we get for investment A, $E = 60$ and for investment B, $E = 50$.[*] As a result, we shall choose investment B. As is already evident, E gives us an average total cost which includes interest q on *fixed* capital. These interest charges, increasing average total cost, influence the choice of 'technological alternative' for producing the desired final effect.

The economic significance of the coefficient of profitability q is the same as the rate of interest. It determines the price for using the fixed capital. The purpose for charging this price is to limit the demand for capital by influencing the choice of methods of production.

A number of criticisms can be raised against this formula.

(1) First of all, the authors of the formula have assumed that the amount of fixed capital is constant during the whole period

[*] $\dfrac{200 + (200 \times 0 \cdot 1 \times 5) + 200}{10} = \dfrac{500}{10} = 50 \quad \dfrac{310 + (310 \times 0 \cdot 1 \times 10) + 90}{12} = \dfrac{710}{12} = 60$

of analysis. Such an assumption is correct only in regard to small and divisible investment, as *e.g.*, increase in the number of trucks. With regard, however, to big, indivisible investment, as *e.g.*, building the new factory, the 'time structure' of fixed capital outlays should be taken into consideration.

(2) Even more serious objections can be raised against the treatment of working capital. Not only is the 'time structure' of working capital disregarded, but there is no charge at all for using the working capital, because the coefficient of profitability q applies to fixed capital only.

(3) We must also note that the investment formula under consideration does not include any charges for the use of natural resources. This, together with the exclusion of working capital from the influence of q, undermines the whole calculation of investment effectiveness. By leaving the working capital and natural resources as 'free goods' (*i.e.*, no interest charges for their use), this investment formula can even stimulate uneconomic substitution between fixed capital and working capital and natural resources in the choice of technological alternatives.

(4) Another possible objection is the fact that the coefficient of profitability q is used in the choice of technological alternatives only, and has no influence on the production costs of a going concern. It is not charged into the costs of production after investment is ready and starts producing output. This practice is a serious obstacle in the rational use of resources.

First of all, the chances of properly choosing technological alternatives with the help of the investment formula are further reduced because of wrong input prices. The sum of investment outlays does not represent the total demand for capital in the branches which supply the given project with the necessary inputs. Some technological alternatives may be more or less 'capital-intensive' than is shown by the investment formula when the derived demand is taken into account. Consequently, certain projects can be chosen as more efficient only because their total capital requirements, including derived demand were not taken into account. Input prices which include the capital charges eliminate this danger. In this last case, the calculation of investment effectiveness includes both direct as well as derived demand for capital required by a given project.

We can also look at the problem of not including interest on capital in cost of production from another standpoint. By a relative lowering of the prices of goods produced by capital-intensive processes in relation to prices of other goods, it increases the demand for them in both production and consumption spheres. As a result, it makes balancing the demand and supply for capital more difficult.

(5) Finally, we may note that a simple rather than compound rate of interest is used. This, however, is not intended as a criticism, because it is our contention that in a socialist economy both types of interest rates can be used, as long as they lead to the desired result: proper influence on the project bureaux in their selection of production methods and help in balancing the supply and demand for capital. In a capitalist economy, compound interest represents the real opportunity costs for the owner of capital, because such an interest rate is paid by the financial institutions, but such considerations are irrelevant in a socialist state which uses the rate of interest only as a tool of economic calculation.

The different critical remarks we have raised against the investment formula under discussion vary in character. Some of them are the result of different 'economic philosophies', as is the case with our postulate of including the price for natural resources in the investment formula and both rent and interest charges in production costs and hence prices of goods. Others, such as considerations of 'time structure' of investment outlays and operational costs, are purely technical but also of great importance for the actual choice of methods of production.

Let us elaborate this last problem by assuming that our investment projects, which we have analysed with the help of the official investment formula, have the following—(a) cost structure, and (b) structure of returns (Table 2).

As we can see from this data, the characteristic features of investment A are: (1) high cost of investment (310), (2) relatively long period of construction—4 years—and (3) small running costs (cost of depreciation is not included). Investment B is the opposite. If we want, however, to explore more deeply the economic characteristics of these investments, we have to introduce two new concepts:

Table 2

Inv. A		1	2	3	4	5	6	7	8	9	10	11	12	13	Total
	years	1	2	3	4	5	6	7	8	9	10	11	12	13	Total
	costs	10	100	100	100	10	10	10	10	10	10	10	10	10	400
	returns	—	—	—	—	50	50	50	50	50	50	50	50	100	500
B	costs	100	100	50	50	50	50	—	—	—	—	—	—	—	400
	returns	—	—	110	110	110	110	—	—	—	—	—	—	—	440

(1) efficiency of investment: $E = \dfrac{R - C}{C}$: where R = total returns and C = total costs, and

(2) period of freezing of means of production Z.

Z = lapse of average returns over investment minus the lapse of average costs over investment.

The lapse of average costs and returns is calculated by using the weighted average:

$$\frac{10 \times 1 + 100 \times 2 + 100 \times 3 \text{ etc.}}{400}$$

When we use the figures from Table No. 1, we receive for investment:

$$A$$
$$E = \frac{500 - 400}{400} = 25\%$$
$$Z = 9 \cdot 4 - 4 \cdot 3 = 5 \cdot 1$$

$$B$$
$$E = \frac{440 - 400}{400} = 10\%$$
$$Z = 4 \cdot 5 - 3 = 1 \cdot 5$$

The above calculations show us the following:

(1) investment A is two and one-half times as efficient as investment B, but

(2) for investment A the enterprise needs credit 400 for 5·1 years, when for investment B the same amount of credit is needed for only 1·5 years.

Whether investment A or B is the more profitable will

depend on the rate of interest charged for investment credits. This is shown in the table below:

Table 3

	Inv. A					Inv. B			
Rate of int.	Costs (without int.)	Compound Interest	Total Costs	Profit (Rev. 500.)	Rate of int.	Cost (without int.)	Compound Interest.	Total Costs	Profit (Rev. 440)
3	400	64	464	36	3	400	18	418	22
3·5	400	76	476	24	3·5	400	21	421	19
4	400	88	488	12	4	400	24	424	16
5	400	112	512	−12	5	400	30	430	10
6	400	138	538	−38	6	400	36	436	4
7	400	165	565	−65	7	400	43	443	−3
8	400	192	592	−92	8	400	48	448	−8

From this table we can see that:

(1) up to 3·7 per cent. investment A is more profitable; above this limit—more profitable is investment B;

(2) investment A is profitable only up to 4·5 per cent., B up to 6·5 per cent.

By choosing the level of rate of interest or the coefficient of profitability q which is used in investment calculation, the Planning Commission can influence the choice of technological alternatives as it does in its original investment formula. The only difference is that now the 'time structure' of total investment outlays and returns is fully taken into account. As a result, in evaluating the effectiveness of the project we consider the real period of freezing of the means of production, or, in other words, the real total demand for capital rather than the partial demand resulting from simplified calculation.

Another method of taking the 'time structure' into account is by discounting with the given interest rate the cost and returns on a given date, e.g. the beginning of the investment project.*

* The relevant formula is the following:

$$P_r = R - C = R_0 - C_0 + \frac{R_1}{\left(1 + \frac{r}{100}\right)} - \frac{C_1}{\left(1 + \frac{r}{100}\right)} + \ldots t \frac{R_n}{\left(1 + \frac{r}{100}\right)^n} - \frac{C_n}{\left(1 + \frac{r}{100}\right)^n}$$

where: P_r = profit, R = returns, C = costs and r = interest rate

The criticism of investment formulae carried out in Polish economic journals did not go unnoticed by the Planning Commission. In 1960, it issued the new 'General Instruction on the Methodology for Analyzing the Economic Efficiency of Investment' (a revised version appeared in 1962). Because, in this new formula, the criticism concerning neglect of the time structure of costs and returns has been met in principle, we shall analyse it only from the point of view of *parameters* used, rather than the functioning of the formula itself. This does not mean that we have no criticism to offer concerning the very construction of the formula. The problem of parameters used is, however, more fundamental as it reflects how the role and function of investment formulae are understood in existing socialist economies.

As we have already said in our general discussion on indices of investment effectiveness in DEC, their main task is to pass on to the project bureaux the requirements of the CPB concerning the methods of production desired at a given stage of economic development. These requirements can be conveniently divided into two groups:

(1) the economical use of capital; the project bureaux have to take into account the scarcity of capital and the employment goals of the plan in elaborating their investment projects, and

(2) the anticipated 'balance scarcity' of different means of production, both domestically produced and imported, must be considered.

Theoretically, these requirements can be met by introducing a price for the use of capital, by charging an interest rate in some form at the level appropriate for the desired 'capital intensity' of the projects, and by price policy for the means of production reflecting their future balance scarcities and hence the prices anticipated when the construction and/or production begins.

With these objectives in mind, let us examine the *parameters* used in investment calculation in Polish planning practice.

Prices of means of production. According to the 'General Instruction . . .' the accounting prices are used only for *imported* inputs. Instead of using prices actually paid by investors to foreign trade enterprises, the accounting price should be used in calculating the effectiveness of investment. This price is fixed at the level of 44 zlotys per dollar for machinery and equipment and 60 zlotys per dollar for raw materials and semi-finished goods.

This use of a high accounting price for imports must be commended. It is obviously consistent both with the task put forth in the Polish perspective plan for 1961–75 of reducing the import of machinery and equipment from 19 per cent. to 8 per cent. of our total imports and with general efforts in our plans to ease the foreign trade barrier, which is the main limiting factor of our growth.

However, the use of a *uniform* accounting price for imports regardless of country of origin does not seem justified. Obviously enough, our import possibilities or, what amounts to the same thing, our possibilities of economically justified export, vary greatly between countries and this should be reflected in our policy of accounting prices for imports. One accounting price for a given category of inputs regardless of its country of origin is not enough for proper guidance of the project bureaux in their choice of methods of production.

According to the 'General Instruction . . .' the domestic means of production are to be valued according to prices current at the time of evaluation of alternative technological variants. The same is true also of the value of expected output. By this rule the CPB is unable to inform the project bureaux about future scarcities.

As a result of the plan, of which a given project is a part, the relative scarcities are going to be changed, frequently changed drastically. These relative changes in scarcity of a given input are, at least, broadly known to the planners. We know for example that at the end of the 5-year plan 1966–70, synthetic materials will be much more abundant, but timber will be as scarce as it is today. But by using *current* prices, this fact will not be communicated to the project bureaux and substitution of plastics for wood will not be encouraged. To take another example, as a result of building a pipeline from the USSR to Poland and a large refinery, the consumption of liquid fuels should be encouraged relative to the present situation in which coal is the main source of fuel in almost all branches of industry. But to reflect this change in emphasis in investment project making, the future rather than current prices of fuel should be used. This, however, is not the present practice and as a result, desired changes in production methods have to be, and are, directly communicated to the project bureaux. But the more elements of methods of production are directly communicated to the project bureaux, the less important becomes the calculation of investment effectiveness, as less and less is left to be decided by such calculation.

Needless to say, what we have said above equally applies to the prices of imported inputs. There, future scarcities are more difficult to predict, but some information is available to the central planners, who do have a long-range plan of foreign trade, partly backed by long-term agreements. And to the extent that such data are available, they should be passed on to the project bureaux in the form of properly differentiated prices. This seems a more reasonable procedure than the exclusive use of accounting prices, even when it is known that the possibility of buying (or selling) on particular markets will deteriorate (or improve) in the next one or two years.

Finally, we have to note that in spite of criticism in the economic journals there is also no price for land in the new investment formula.

Prices for the use of capital. The current investment formula* uses a number of coefficients which are charged as costs for different parts of capital outlays or are used as a discount rate

---

* The current investment formula reads as follows:

$$E = \frac{\frac{1}{T} \times I(1 + q_z \times n_z) + Kst \times Yn}{Pst \times Z_n} + \frac{O_s \times q_s}{P}$$

where:

E = efficiency of investment
T = the required recoupment period
I = investment costs
q_z = coefficient of 'freezing up' of fixed capital
n_z = the construction period
Kst = constant yearly prime costs (minus depreciation plus maintenance costs)

for expected returns. Thus, we have the following coefficients:

T = the required recoupment period
q_z = coefficient of 'freezing up' of fixed capital
q_s = coefficient of 'freezing up' of working capital
Y_n = coefficient correcting the prime costs and
Z_n = coefficient correcting the volume of output.

The numerical values of these coefficients are fixed by the Planning Commission. The 'General Instruction . . .' (revised version) sets them at the following levels: $T=6$, $q_z=16$ per cent., $q_s=12$ per cent., and Y_n and Z_n are calculated with the help of a discount rate of 4 per cent. and 7 per cent. respectively and the concept of so-called 'standard period of useful life of investment' fixed as 20 years.*

Quite apart from possible objections to constructing the formula with different charges for fixed capital and for working capital and different discount rates for costs and returns, thus making a proper evaluation of investment projects impossible, one can question the basis on which the level of these different coefficients was fixed. I do not want to question the exact numerical value of these coefficients but rather the methodological assumptions which lie behind fixing their level.

Only in fixing the level of T, the recoupment period, did the authors of the 'General Instruction . . .' approach the problem

* See footnote on p. 44.

Y_n = coefficient correcting the prime costs. (It is calculated according to the following formula:

$$Y_n = \frac{1 - \left(\frac{1}{1+c}\right)^n}{1 - \left(\frac{1}{1+c}\right)^{n_s}}$$

It is the ratio of costs of the investment project with the non-standard period of useful life (n) to the costs of the investment project with the standard period of useful life ($n_s=20$) (c is the discount rate $=4$ per cent.).

O_s = the volume of working capital
q_s = coefficient of 'freezing up' of working capital
Pst = constant yearly volume of output
Z_n = coefficient correcting the volume of output. (It is calculated according to the same formula what Y_n, but instead of discount rate of 4 per cent. (c), the 7 per cent. discount (a) is applied.)
P = volume of output.

explicitly from the viewpoint of the needs of the plan. Thus we learn that the basic condition which determines the optimal level of the recoupment period is the necessity of aiming at a technical level of investment which would most increase the national income from given investment funds and labour force. In other words, the coefficient $1/T$ used in the investment formula has to influence the average level of capital-intensity of investment projects and, as a result, limit the demand for investment funds to the level of its planned supply.

But obviously enough, the choice of technological alternatives depends on the total result of investment calculations, and this is influenced not only by a prescribed recoupment period but also by the other coefficients used in investment calculations: q_z, q_s and Y_n and Z_n. The level of these coefficients, however, was fixed not with a view to bringing about a level of capital-intensity desired at a given stage of economic development, nor with a view to checking effectively the tendency, which is very likely to occur in the project bureaux of elaborating the technically best methods of production without due regard to scarcity of capital and the employment goals of the plan. Instead, it was fixed at the level corresponding to certain macroeconomic relationships, without any effort whatsoever to examine the total effect of such determined coefficients on the choice of methods of production. For instance, the level of q_z corresponds to the efficiency of investment funds in the past, the discount rate for prime costs at 4 per cent. is the difference between the average growth rate of national income (7 per cent.) and the average rate of diminishing costs of production due to increased efficiency (3 per cent.) and the level of the discount rate for returns was fixed at the level corresponding to average yearly growth of production. Obviously, all these magnitudes are external to the plan itself and there is no theoretical reason to expect that their joint application in calculating the economic effectiveness of technological alternatives will lead to the desired results of eliminating inefficient projects so that total supply and demand for investment funds will be balanced, even if this balancing is done for individual sectors rather than for the national economy as a whole.

It seems to us that, if investment formulae are going to be efficient tools by which the Central Planners may influence the elaboration of production methods by the projects bureaux, the level of the rate of interest or any of its equivalents (co-efficient of profitability, recoupment period, etc.) has to be directly fixed in accord with the situation envisaged by the plan and then tested empirically. At present they reflect certain macro-economic relationships, whose use as determinants of the level of interest rate cannot be justified on analytical or empirical grounds.

To this we may add that a *simple* investment formula is always better than a complicated one, provided that it accounts for all elements of the so-called 'investment problem'. This is especially true in relation to the number of different coefficients used in the formula. The use of many rates of interest cannot be analytically justified; in addition it raises the problem of evaluating their *joint* influence on the choice of project. Instead of finding a single rate of interest which will lead to desired results, one has to find an optimal combination of them and to predict the probable effects of changes of any one of the coefficients. Since, as we shall soon see, one has enough troubles with a complex incentive system, it is better not to begin experimenting with complex coefficients in the invest-ment formula. Experience shows that the final results of such complex formulae are difficult to predict. Hence, their opera-tional value as a management tool is substantially lowered.

REFERENCES

[1] M. Kalecki, An Outline of a Method of Constructing a Per-spective Plan (based on Polish Experience), in 'Essays on Plan-ning and Economic Development', Warsaw, 1963, pp. 19–21.

THE ECONOMIC TOOLS
OF PLAN FULFILMENT: I*

Introductory remarks. The problem of plan fulfilment, as
we see it, is the problem of constructing a mechanism for
stimulating producers and consumers to pursue planned goals.
This mechanism, in turn, can be divided, somewhat artificially,
into two parts: the economic and the social tools of plan
fulfilment, the latter dealing with management through social
integration. Here, we shall be concerned with the economic
tools of plan fulfilment in relation to producers only. Furthermore, we shall confine our discussion to incentives for managerial staff.

We propose to call the economic tools of plan fulfilment
'the formula for the management of the socialist economy',
or just the 'formula' for short. Every formula can be divided
into three main components: incentives (both material and
non-material), prices, and methods of accounting (which
include cost calculation). As an example, let us take a formula
where the incentive is in the form of a bonus based on profit.
To give this incentive any operational value, three things must
be decided: rules of price fixing (*e.g.*, cost-plus, MC pricing,
etc.), the methods of accounting (including cost calculation,
rules concerning what constitutes gross and net revenue,
depreciation rules, etc.), and finally rules concerning calculation
of the bonus itself.

This approach considers incentives, prices, and methods of
accounting as the three basic elements of the mechanism for

* This is a slightly revised version of Professor A. Wakar's and my article
'Socialist Operational Price Systems', American Economic Review, March
1963.

plan fulfilment. The characteristic feature of this approach is the stress laid on the unity of these elements, on their mutual interdependence.

The main conclusions which can be drawn from this interdependence between prices, incentives, and methods of accounting are as follows:

(1) The operational price and incentive systems always have to be analysed together and not in isolation. Isolated analysis, however, is usually practised by planning authorities and also appears in many economic writings. It is rarely recognized that for every incentive system there is an appropriate price system (and also an appropriate method of accounting) and that the changes in one element of the formula have to be accompanied by compensating changes in the others. Otherwise, there will be a contradiction between prices and incentives used, a contradiction from the point of view of their influence on plan fulfilment.

(2) With direct economic calculation there is no optimal price or incentive system *per se*. However, we can find their optimal combination—that combination which best serves plan fulfilment and which precludes price or incentive stimuli not in harmony with planned tasks.

(3) The 'price consequences' of any incentive system or of contemplated changes in it (for instance, changes in rules and/or intensity of incentives) must always be carefully analysed to avoid possible negative effects on plan fulfilment. And conversely, any price changes must be analysed from the standpoint of their impact on the functioning of the given incentive system.

(4) The choice of any given incentive system determines the system of operational prices which can be effectively used in conjunction with it (and vice versa). This mutual interdependence of the incentive and operational price system limits the CPB's freedom of action in making both price and incentive policy.

To prove these conclusions we shall analyse the interdependencies between prices and three main types of incentive systems used or discussed in a socialist economy, namely, gross output incentives, profit incentives, and value-added incentives.

Gross output incentives and prices. Until very recently, the most widely used incentive for managers of enterprises in socialist countries was a bonus for fulfilling the plan of gross value of output (valovaya produktsiya). An appraisal in value terms requires that output be aggregated according to specified rules. In practice, aggregates are calculated in money terms, and prices are, as a rule, equal to the average total cost of the branch of industry plus a given percentage of profit.

The experience of socialist countries has shown beyond any doubt that bonuses for fulfilling (and overfulfilling) the plan of gross output have had decidedly negative effects on socialist production, the more so because of existing pricing practices. The current method of pricing (average total cost of the branch of industry plus 5 per cent. profit) tends to approximate the value relations between different products. Product A which requires twice as much resources as product B is also twice as expensive. By pricing in this manner, the Central Planning Board attempts to limit the demand for product A in production and consumption and tries to encourage the demand for product B. It is easy to see, however, that so long as gross output bonuses are paid and current pricing practices are adhered to, managers will not follow the intentions of the Central Planning Board because it is to their advantage to choose expensive inputs and to substitute product A for product B [3, pp. 155–66]. We may label this a case of 'Gresham's Law in reverse'. Therefore, when a bonus system for fulfilling the gross output plan and a system of average cost-plus pricing are used together, they disorganize socialist production. In order to remedy this contradiction, either the price system has to be adjusted to the incentive system which is being used, or the incentive system must be made compatible with average cost-plus pricing.

If for the sake of argument we disregard practical difficulties and the prevailing way of thinking in regard to price ratios, we may consider changes in the price system as theoretically feasible. We want to stress, however, that in the end we shall not propose that the gross output bonus system be 'improved' by adjusting the system of pricing in an appropriate manner. We merely want to point out those changes in the price system which must be made if gross output bonuses are to be used effectively as an incentive device for plan fulfilment.

First, let us determine the buyer prices which would induce buyers (enterprises) to meet the objectives of the Central Planning Board.* If we want to prevent enterprises from over-fulfilling the plan for, say, 100 per cent. woollen cloth at the expense of 40 per cent. woollen cloth, it would be advisable to equalize the prices of 100 per cent. woollen yarn and of 40 per cent. woollen yarn. The smaller the price difference between various grades of yarn, the less the danger that enterprises will violate their assortment plan. The conclusion that in order to prevent enterprises from taking the easy way out, input prices must be similar or identical applies especially to raw materials, since their value is transferred into the product during one production process. But it also applies to machinery and equipment. The higher the depreciation rates and the share of depreciation allowances in total cost, the more pressing is the need for price equalization.

Second, let us look at the seller prices which would lead sellers to meet the objectives of the Central Planning Board. In order to render gross output incentives effective, only the prices of inputs have to be equalized. Different types of output (*e.g.*, ordinary watches and waterproof plus shock-resistant watches, dacron suits and woollen suits, etc.) usually require different production processes and different production expenditures. If enterprises are to be induced to fulfil their production plans under these conditions, prices for different kinds of output have to take these facts into account. If we

* The buyers are here, of course, the state enterprises and not the individual consumers. We are concerned in this lecture with so-called 'operational prices' only, which are used within the socialist sector for stimulating producers—sellers and buyers—to plan fulfilment. In the socialist economy there are also so-called 'programming prices' used for construction of the plan and so-called 'consumers' prices', which have to equalize supply and demand, and at the same time, to influence consumption patterns in the direction socially desirable (as seen by the Central Planning Board). See Lecture Three: 'The Direct Economic Calculation' and Lecture Nine: 'The Consumption Model and the Tools of Its Implementation'.

were to apply the policy of equal prices to seller prices, we
would put a premium on assortments with a small share of
value added because they can be produced more easily. If
seller prices were made proportional to average total cost,
input prices being the same, we would still put a similarly
undesirable, however smaller, premium on assortments with
smaller share of value added. To avoid this consequence, we
have to find a price ratio that would discourage enterprises
from concentrating on assortments which are easy to produce
and hence which yield larger gross output bonuses. Such a
seller price ratio has to equal the ratio of value added.

For illustration, we may use a numerical example of ordinary
watches and waterproof plus shock-resistant watches. The
temptation to utilize expensive inputs has been eliminated by
equalizing input prices, and it is assumed that the material input
is the same in quantitative terms. Thus production costs differ
only because of the difference in value added.

Table 4

	Ordinary Watch	Waterproof Shock-resistant Watch
Average transferred value	10	10
Average value added	10	20
Average total cost	20	30

If we assume that a given enterprise can produce a maximum
of 1000 units of value added, then the influence of choice of
assortment on gross output varies with different seller prices.

Table 5

	Volume of Gross Output Depending on Assortment Chosen	
	Ordinary Watch	Waterproof Watch
Equal seller prices /30:30/	3000	1500
Average cost pricing /20:30/	2000	1500
Value added prices /20:40/	2000	2000

To avoid favouring either the production of ordinary watches or the production of waterproof, shock-resistant watches, our price ratio would have to equal the ratio of value added.

We have thus far found certain rules for price-setting within the framework of gross output incentives. Buyer (input) prices, as a rule, are to be equalized. Thus we eliminate the incentive to use expensive means of production as an easy method of fulfilling the gross output plan. Equalized buyer prices, however, do not solve the assortment problem. For its satisfactory resolution, seller prices have to be set so that they cover (industrial) average total cost plus 'society's share' (accruing to the state, *e.g.*, in the form of turnover tax) and so that seller price ratios equal the ratios of value added.

Within the framework of gross output incentives, these methods of pricing can be used effectively by the Central Planning Board as instruments of economic policy in affecting methods as well as directions of production, since they enable the Central Planning Board to strengthen administrative orders with material incentives. So far as methods of production are concerned, the Central Planning Board can induce any branch of industry to use desired inputs by increasing the prices of these inputs. In the case of machinery and equipment, demand also depends on depreciation rates and on rates of interest for fixed capital. By raising these rates, the Central Planning Board can further stimulate demand for machinery and equipment. So far as direction of production is concerned, the Central Planning Board can induce enterprises to exert special efforts in producing certain products or kinds of products by fixing the ratio of seller prices appropriately in their favour. Generally speaking, equal buyer prices are 'neutral' in the sense that they induce indifference between inputs. And seller price ratios, equal to value added ratios, are 'neutral' in the sense that they induce indifference between outputs. In the case of neutral price ratios, the Central Planning Board has to rely on administrative orders only. Any deviation from these neutral price ratios, however, provides an incentive in a particular direction, and price differentiation can thus be used by the Central Planning Board as a tool of economic policy.

Although we thus can discover prices which 'neutralize' or 'balance' the negative influence of gross output bonuses on the fulfilment of assortment plans for inputs as well as for outputs, there are serious objections to the implementation of such a system of prices:

1. The required price structure violates so-called common sense. The prices of goods which 'everywhere and always' were and are expensive (*e.g.*, 100 per cent. woollen yarn) would have to be equal to the prices of relatively cheap goods (*e.g.*, 40 per cent. woollen yarn). The prices of goods bought and sold within the state sector would have to be fixed at ratios which would deviate far from these which we are accustomed to view as proper. The habit of thinking that price ratios have to, or ought to correspond to the 'value' ratios cannot be overcome easily. Adherence to this habit is not astonishing in view of the several thousand years of experience from which it has been formed [2, App. I by F. Engels]. Indeed, one may even wonder whether this habit can be overcome at all. For this reason, it may be better to look for an incentive system which would be compatible with the more 'traditional' price system.

2. Within the framework of gross output incentives, we cannot induce the effective use of resources, even if prices are manipulated in the way suggested, because the system as such does not provide incentives for 'economizing' in the sense of minimizing the use of manpower and of capital. This deficiency is attributable to the fact that the enterprises are required to maximize gross output. By fixing prices appropriately as described previously, we may be able to eliminate many of the negative allocative effects of the gross output incentive system, but we do not create incentives for improving the technical production coefficients. Within the framework of gross output incentives, we cannot expect 'initiative from below' on the part of enterprises and/or branches of industry with a view to economizing the use of means of production. When prices are given, economizing has to be induced from above, for instance in the form of plan targets for cost reductions, input norms, etc.★

★ In practice, gross output incentives are usually supplemented by incentives to economize inputs per unit of output, *e.g.*, in the form of bonuses for

3. Within the framework of gross output incentives, we cannot avoid using two different price systems within the socialist sector, *viz.*, a buyer price system and a seller price system. This requirement, however, holds true for other incentive systems as well, as we shall see in the following sections.

4. The practical difficulties of devising and operating a price system which is compatible with gross output incentives are evidently enormous. In view of the other objections to such a price system, it does not seem worth the effort necessary to implement it.

The aim of our analysis is not, however, to defend the system of gross output incentives, but to derive requirements for an effective price system corresponding to it. As a by-product of this discussion, the relativity of the law of supply and demand has become conspicuously apparent. Such obvious relationships as that between price and demand (the higher the price, the smaller the demand) hold true, in fact, only under certain institutional arrangements. Changes in the system of stimulating producers (*e.g.*, a change to gross output incentives) affect the relation between price and demand (*e.g.*, in the case of gross output incentives, an increase in the price of an input will increase the demand for that input). However obvious this fact may be, it is worthwhile to emphasize that a given relation depends upon a given institutional setting, because of the tremendous power of habit which is connected with that relation. Habit of thought is probably the main factor which explains why the Central Planning Board has made use of, and continues to make some use of, gross output incentives in combination with more or less 'normal' price ratios and why it has practised a price policy which has assumed more or less 'traditional' price-demand relations.

Profit incentives and prices. At the present time only a few economists would defend an incentive system based on gross

---

diminishing unit cost. For the time being, however, we do not analyse the 'mixed' incentive systems with bonuses based on many targets, as, *e.g.*, achievements in raising the level of gross output, diminishing unit costs, improving the quality of products, introducing technical developments, etc. These problems are analysed in Lecture Eight.

output. Rather, the profit-sharing system for workers and bonuses based on profit for management are advocated. The incentive system based on profit also consists of three parts: (1) bonuses based on profit achieved (or planned), and (2) a system of prices for means of production and final goods which together with (3) given methods of accounting are designed to determine the relative profitability of individual enterprises and branches of industry.

Can there be contradictions between profit incentives and the existing price system? Very likely yes. Only one (or a few) price systems can stimulate enterprises to behave in accordance with plans as to 'what' and 'how' to produce; and the existing system of operational prices does not meet the necessary requirements.

Within the framework of profit incentives, the system of operational prices bears some resemblance to the system of prices under 'market socialism' of the Lange-Lerner type, except for these fundamental differences:

1. In the theoretical model of market socialism prices constitute an internally consistent system which, on the one hand, enables the CPB to achieve the optimal allocation of resources, and on the other, in conjunction with bonuses based on profit, stimulates enterprises to work towards plan fulfilment.

In existing socialist countries which are using the method of direct economic calculation (DEC), the prices together with profit incentives have to stimulate the enterprises to plan fulfilment. However, as we have argued elsewhere (see Lecture Five and References [5], [6, pp. 83–91], [7]), prices cannot be, and are not, used for economic verification of technical coefficients, but they can and have to be used to enforce the universal application of methods of production that the CPB deems appropriate. Both in the theoretical market socialism model and in DEC, operational prices coupled with a given incentive system have an empirical character. They have to be adjusted according to the supply-demand situation and must not be based on any *a priori* rule of price determination (*e.g.*, average total costs of branch of industry plus 5 per cent. profit).

2. In theoretical market socialism there is only one price

facing both buyers and sellers. This is one of the basic requirements of this model. The one-price principle is essential for
achieving the technical efficiency of production. Different
prices for a given good exist only in the sphere of consumption.
With DEC, the situation is quite different, for the one-price
principle is not one of its cornerstones. It seems to us that the
principle of double prices—different for buyers and sellers—
must be adhered to, if prices are to be used effectively as part
of the incentive system.

Let us begin with the prices of means of production. The
necessity for two different systems of operational prices, one
for buyers and one for sellers, is the result of the external
character of production methods in DEC. Because of the
external character of methods of production there is little
reason to expect that one price can properly stimulate both
sellers and buyers to follow the methods of production prescribed for them in the national plan. These planned methods
of production are not internally consistent in the national
economy as a whole and are not fully co-ordinated with the price
structure. The latter evolved historically; among its many
antecedents were the efforts to use prices to stimulate increased
production in bottleneck areas.

In such a situation one should not be astonished by rather
general contradictions between methods of production prescribed by the CPB and the methods of production implied (and
stimulated) by relative prices. To resolve these contradictions
one needs a double-price system which differentiates between
producers and users, or a turnover tax calculated to achieve the
same result.

The contradiction of the interests of sellers and buyers can
apply to the general price level as well as to the individual prices
of means of production.

In the sphere of consumers' goods there is also a need for
different prices for sellers and buyers (the latter are now individual consumers). Two main reasons for this need are:

I. The CPB is, as a rule, active in the sphere of individual
consumption. It has definite preferences regarding the desired
structure of consumption because of social welfare and other

considerations. In effectuating this policy, within the framework of free consumers' choice, the level and the structure of consumer goods' prices play an important role. As long as the total volume of consumer demand does not call for an amount of resources in excess of that allocated to industries producing consumers' goods, in a planned economy there are no serious reasons for the CPB—irrespective of the type of economic calculation actually applied—to be constrained in its consumer goods price policy by the level and structure of the costs of production of individual commodities. There are no persuasive reasons for 'cost fetishism' in any type of economic calculation because the costs of production are more or less incidental, as incidental as the level and pace of technical progress in different branches of production, factor endowment in a given country, etc.*

   2. If it is true that there are no valid reasons for cost fetishism under any method of economic calculation, it is especially true under DEC. As we have argued elsewhere, [5] [7] in DEC the price ratios, as a rule, do not reflect marginal rates of transformation. Costs based on these prices, then, obviously must also deviate from marginal rates of transformation. In such a situation it would be a serious mistake to allow the cost structure (via retail prices) to influence the structure of consumption.†

* Of course, consumers' sovereignty is abolished here. But let us assume for the moment that differences in price ratios between say, Poland and the United States as shown in Table 6, are the result of real differences in marginal cost ratios. Would it not be risky to say that one or the other structure of consumption, resulting, *ceteris paribus*, from the given price structure, is better than the other ? If there are no objective criteria to determine what structure of consumption is better than another, the CPB has no reason to be much worried that, because of random elements in the consumer price structure, it is doing any harm. Moreover, in many cases it has definite opinions about the desired structure (and volume) of consumption, and price policy allows it to achieve its objectives without limiting the freedom of consumers' choice [6, pp. 134–75] [7, pp. 100–2].

Table 6
Retail Price Ratios (1961)

	U.S.A.	Poland
Ready-made suit—one lb. of ham	50:1	60:1
Can of sardines—one telephone call	2:1	40:1
Cup of coffee—tram ticket	0·5:1	10:1
Drip-dry shirt—scientific book	1:1	18:1
Stretch socks—cinema ticket	1:1	4:1

   † Elements which have to be considered to determine the level and structure of retail prices are discussed in (4, pp. 65–78) and (6, pp. 134–70, 179–90).

We have said above that within the framework of DEC two systems of operational prices are needed for the effective use of prices as a part of a profit-incentive system. Let us discuss them in more detail and also introduce the concept of 'margin of tolerance' which, in many cases, may render different prices for buyers and sellers unnecessary. The margin of tolerance can be defined as an area around the existing price within which price changes for buyers and/or sellers do not induce the enterprises to change existing methods of production and product-mix. As long as the margins of tolerance of buyers' prices (P_b) and sellers' prices (P_s) are overlapping, the need for a system of two distinct sets of operational prices does not exist.

The magnitude of the margin of tolerance in different product groups and in the same product group, in different enterprises of buyers and sellers, may vary. The very existence and actual magnitude of the margin of tolerance is a result of several factors:

1. Differentiated pressure of administrative orders. In DEC one of the main reasons for the existence of the margin of tolerance is the system of administrative orders—quantitative ('What to produce'?) influencing P_s, and qualitative ('How to produce') influencing P_b. Under the system of administrative orders any deviation from planned tasks, not resulting from factors beyond the enterprise's power, represents an illegal act. This undoubtedly inhibits deviations from the plan that may arise from the desire for material gains. The size of the margin of tolerance attributable to administrative orders depends in part on the actual pressure of administrative orders. As we know from experience, the actual pressure of administrative orders usually differs by branches of industry and by product groups. It is especially great in branches or products of so-called 'high priority'.

2. Achieved level of social integration also has an influence on the magnitude of the margin of tolerance. Under *ceteris paribus* assumptions, the magnitude of the margin of tolerance is proportional to the achieved level of social integration. A high level of social integration means that the producers

identify the planned goals with their own and therefore do their best to achieve them even if the actual price structure makes certain deviations profitable.

3. The absolute and relative magnitude of financial gains realizable by plan deviation obviously constitutes an important parameter determining the magnitude of the margin of tolerance. The pay-offs of plan deviation depend on many variables —among others, on the relative share of bonuses in the total income of management personnel. In the situation, not unknown in Poland a few years ago, in which bonuses ran as high as 50–60 per cent. of total income and are indispensable for maintaining a 'normal' standard of living, the natural tendency on the part of management to obtain bonuses (almost regardless of consequences) substantially diminishes the actual margin of tolerance. Under other circumstances, with different incentive intensities, the margin of tolerance would be substantially greater.

4. The existence of the 'insensitivity margin'. The magnitude of the margin of tolerance depends also on several factors which we can denominate as the 'insensitivity margin'. (a) First of all, there is the relative share of a given input in total costs. If the share of a given input in total costs is in the range of one or a few per cent., the 'sensitivity' of the enterprise (or the branch of industry) to its price change is, as a rule, small. If a certain input comprises, say, 1 per cent. of total costs, even a 20 per cent. increase in its price will lead to only a 0·2 per cent. increase in total cost. It is very probable that a total cost increase of this magnitude will not cause any realignments in enterprise demand, and so the given price increase lies within the margin of tolerance. If, on the other hand, the very same input comprises 20 per cent. of total costs, the same price increase can initiate the process of substitution. We can conclude, therefore, that the margin of tolerance for any commodity is differentiated according to individual enterprises, buyers or sellers. That is, the *effective* margin of tolerance is a magnitude of price change which does not cause deviation from planned performance in any enterprise. It is determined by the smallest margin of tolerance, *i.e.*, the margin of tolerance in the branch

or enterprise with the narrowest insensitivity margin. This obviously complicates the task of constructing a system of uniform prices for buyers and sellers but nevertheless it enables the CPB to construct a system of double prices (P_b and P_s) instead of individual accounting prices for every enterprise. (b) The further element which accounts for the existence of the insensitivity margin and, via this margin, influences the magnitude of the margin of tolerance, is routine. Because of routine, price changes within certain limits do not have any effect on the demand or supply schedules of enterprises. This unwillingness to change has its subjective aspect—any change means as a rule effort and trouble for enterprise management; and its objective aspect—usually every change costs money (the cost of changing technology, input norms, machine operations, etc.).

5. Lack of substitutes. Another factor which affects the existence and magnitude of the margin of tolerance is the substitutability of the different means of production. The more specialized a given means of production, the less sensitive the enterprise is to a change in its price and the greater the margin of tolerance. However, the ease of substituting input A varies with different enterprises. Input A may be easy to substitute in producing X, and very difficult in producing Z. Here again we meet the effective margin of tolerance described above.

Thus far we have been discussing substitutability in the strict sense, *i.e.*, as determined by technical causes, and we have come to the conclusion that the smaller the substitutability the greater the margin of tolerance and vice versa (of course under *ceteris paribus* assumptions). Substitutability can also be limited (the margin of tolerance increased) administratively, by rationing. The rationing of means of production, which means that the enterprise cannot buy, say, brick and lumber in other proportions than those prescribed by the plan, or cannot buy more of any of these inputs than the planned allotment, has the same effect as technical insubstitutability and diminishes the enterprise's sensitivity to price changes, *i.e.*, increases the margin of tolerance.

The possibility of substitution acts counter to the margin of tolerance, because it creates the objective basis for deviation from quantitative and qualitative planned tasks. The motive, however, for taking advantage of substitution possibilities is financial gain (in the form of profit bonuses) which can be achieved as the result of unauthorized changes in plan fulfilment. If the possibility of substitution is limited by technological and institutional (rationing) factors, the profitability of substitution, within these limits, depends on the price ratios. The margin of tolerance around the price of input A depends then, among other things, on the profitability of its substitution by or for input B, *i.e.*, on the price ratio of substitutes. Hence the margin of tolerance around a given price depends on the price system.

The price system, however, does not determine the magnitude of the margin of tolerance, but only its distribution around a given price. Let us assume, for example, that the price ratio of lignite and coal is 1:2 and that, with their prices fixed at 10:20, the margin of tolerance is symmetrical and identical for both prices at the 10 per cent. level; that is, in this case the margin of tolerance = price ± 10 per cent. The change in the price ratio to 9:22 will make the margin of tolerance asymmetric for both prices, and moreover, the margin of tolerance will exist now only in the case of a price increase for lignite (+20 per cent.) and for a price decrease for coal (−20 per cent.). In constructing the system of operational prices we have to take this into account.

The existence of the margin of tolerance creates the objective basis for fixing one price for both buyers and sellers, in spite of the external character of methods of production, without the danger of active, negative influence of prices on plan fulfilment. The possibility of fixing one price exists when the effective margins of tolerance around P_b and P_s are overlapping.

The effective margin of tolerance can be extended or contracted as a result of the CPB's economic policy. One reason why the CPB may be interested in extending the margin of tolerance is the desire to have one price for both buyers and sellers in the greatest possible number of cases. In changing the margin of tolerance the CPB can rely on: (1) the varying intensity of administrative orders, (2) differentiating the share of bonuses (based on profit) in absolute terms and in relation to basic salaries, and (3) rationing policy. With (a) strong administrative orders and (b) limited bonuses, it is possible, in a great number of cases, to fix one price both for buyers and sellers.

At the same time we have to realize that action by the CPB to increase the margin of tolerance has also its negative aspect because, in its ultimate effects, it means diminishing the force of incentives: directly diminishing it when we consciously limit the possible absolute and relative magnitude of financial gains which can be obtained by management; indirectly diminishing it when we rely on administrative orders and rationing of the means of production. Diminishing the force of material incentives at a given level of social integration means the actual deterioration of average performance.

The margin of tolerance is a feature of the price system which is not unique to socialist economies. It also exists in capitalist economies. However, as far as we know, it is usually not taken into account in texts on price theory. The existence of the margin of tolerance in capitalist economies is not surprising, because most of its sources are not specific characteristics of socialist economies, and with few exceptions (administrative orders and rationing) are present in market economies as well. We are also inclined to think—though this is still only a guess which needs substantial research for its verification—that the margin of tolerance is present especially in big enterprises. In big enterprises the sources of the margin of tolerance (specifically, the insensitivity margin) are especially strong. (In a big enterprise the cost and time involved in adapting to price changes are particularly great and hence the profitability of reacting to every price change, however small, is apt to be less than in smaller business units.)

At this stage of our analysis we can formulate several conclusions:

1. There are many 'equilibrium' price systems for a given plan.

2. Because of the margin of tolerance the CPB can in many cases fix one price for both sellers and buyers, in spite of the

external character of the methods of production under direct economic calculation.

3. The existence of the margin of tolerance facilitates the stabilization of operational prices without negative effects on plan fulfilment. As long as changes in economic conditions (and thus in planned tasks) call for a change in prices within their margins of tolerance, keeping prices unchanged by definition does not cause any reaction by enterprises and does not weaken incentives to any substantial degree. Keeping prices stable, therefore, has no adverse effects on plan fulfilment.

When we discussed the price system required for an incentive system based on gross output, we felt a little like Alice in Wonderland. It was the economic world as we know it topsy-turvy: expensive products were priced the same as cheap goods, price increases had the effect of increasing effective demand, etc. Within the framework of profit incentives such an extraordinary price system is not necessary for effective plan fulfilment. Because the goal of the enterprise is now profit rather than gross output, it is possible to use prices based on the notion of production costs and to have a more or less traditional price structure. Scarce goods, which have to be economized, can again command high prices and vice versa. Of course, we are only saying here that now prices can be related to production costs, not that there is any rigid formula by which they should be determined. If profit bonuses are to be used as an effective incentive for fulfilling planned tasks, the prices must have an empirical character, to be fixed and changed according to varying economic conditions and plan objectives.

This empirical approach to prices is in direct contradiction to the general and deeply rooted tendency of 'price fetishism'. The experience of capitalist economies has accustomed us to think that prices must be based on value, price of production, or costs. This is the root of the belief that prices have to be 'proper', that is to say, they must have an objective basis in costs, however calculated. It would be in direct contradiction to this belief to fix a high price for low-cost goods or vice versa. The empirical approach is limited by fetishism.

Value-added incentives and prices. The incentive system based on gross output stimulates enterprises to use expensive instead of cheap methods of production and to produce material-intensive rather than labour-intensive goods. The change from the incentive system based on gross output to one based on value added eliminates, to a great extent, the negative influence of 'normal' prices (*i.e.*, prices based on average cost of production plus 5 per cent. profit) upon plan fulfilment. At the same time, however, it creates certain new problems dangerous for the effective functioning of the national economy.

By value added is meant here the difference between gross output and the value of all material means of production, interest, rent, and taxes. This definition of value added is used for the purpose of economic policy and differs from the definition of value added *sensu stricto* as used in Marxian economic theory. In the latter sense the value added is equal to $v+s$ (variable capital plus surplus value) and obviously includes wages, interest, rent, taxes, and similar forms of redistribution of value added.

Within the framework of the incentive system, based on value added as defined above, the enterprises will use means of production according to their price ratios fixed by the CPB. Because the values of these inputs do not directly influence the value added, there is no reason for the enterprises to prefer expensive inputs in choosing production methods. There is also no reason for them to try to overfulfil the plan of gross output by eliminating the cheap goods from their assortment plan.

How will enterprises behave under the incentive system based on value added ?

A. Methods of production

With given prices the enterprises will try to minimize the 'transferred value' (*i.e.*, value of constant capital) and other items which are subtracted from gross output, because this, *ex definitione*, will help to maximize their value added. The CPB can stimulate enterprises to economize any given input by a relative rise of its price or vice versa.

Whether the enterprises will economize the capital stock depends on the type of cost calculation used. Under the cost calculation which does not include interest charges and rent, there will be a tendency on the part of enterprises to have as large a capital stock as possible. The latter does not cost them much (only depreciation charges which, thus far, are very small in most socialist countries) and it facilitates the maximization of value added. This tendency, however, can be avoided by charging a proper interest rate and rent, and by a sound depreciation policy. Under this type of cost calculation it will be profitable for enterprises, trying to maximize value added, to use the capital stock and natural resources only to a certain level. The CPB can raise or lower this level by appropriate changes in interest and rent charges.

Using an incentive system based on value added, we can expect the initiative for economizing the material means of production to come from within the enterprise. Whether this initiative will also lead to an attempt to economize capital stock and natural resources will depend on the type of cost calculation used.

This rosy picture of incentives based on value added also, however, has its negative side: the impact on labour force utilization and thus on the utilization of material means of production. Within the framework of incentives based on value added the labour force has a zero or even negative price from the point of view of its influence on the level of value added. Let us assume that the production plan of the enterprise is 10 units of X at 10 zlotys per unit in operational prices, and that planned costs are:

Materials and depreciation	80
Wages and salaries (value added)	20
Total	100

with 10 per cent. bonus for achieving the planned volume of value added.

If the enterprise achieves the production target, using a labour input 10 per cent. higher than planned (*e.g.*, due to overtime work), the level of value added will not be influenced. Bonuses will therefore not be diminished. In this situation, from the point of view of the enterprise, the marginal cost of labour is zero.

If the enterprise achieves the production target, using a labour input 10 per cent. higher than planned (*e.g.*, due to overtime work), but at the same time cutting non-labour inputs by 5 units, it will overfulfil the value-added plan. In this case, the labour force has a negative price from the point of view of bonus maximization. The same will hold, only not so strongly, if the use of more labour input than planned is due to additional employment (and not overtime) since then the bonuses will have to be shared by a greater number of employees. This will also be true, even more strongly, under a system of progressive bonuses based on value added.

The result is that within the framework of incentives based on value added there will be a tendency on the part of enterprises to substitute labour for material means of production. There will also be a lack of financial incentives to economize labour.

Two serious dangers are connected with this: (1) the danger of spending more on the national wage fund than planned, resulting in a disequilibrium in the consumers' goods market, leading to inflationary pressure; and (2) the danger that deviations from planned methods of production will disturb the planned real-balance equilibrium, *i.e.*, relationships envisaged in the national input-output table.

Can these dangers be prevented by an appropriate price policy? Obviously not. In the situation where the price of labour from the enterprise's point of view is zero or negative, there is no possible change in the price ratios of material means of production to labour which can remedy the two dangers mentioned above. The remedy lies in administrative means. Price policy *per se* is ineffective. But used in conjunction with administrative means it can again become an effective tool in stimulating producers to fulfil planned tasks. To achieve this, we have to eliminate the zero or negative price of the labour at the enterprise level. It can be done by strict control and rationing of the wage fund.

Under strict rationing of the wage fund, when the enterprise cannot increase its value added by increasing labour inputs, labour ceases to have a zero or negative price in enterprise calculation. When this is the case, price policy for material means of production is again an effective tool for stimulating producers to achieve the planned methods of production and product-mix. Enterprises treat labour inputs as given (a function of the planned wage fund) and react to changes in price ratios in the same way as under profit incentives, *i.e.*, they try to equate the marginal value productivity of each factor with its price. The CPB can again use the prices of factors of production as a part of an incentive system.

We have to realize, however, that value-added incentives create a certain conflict of interest between enterprises and the Central Planning Board. At the stage of plan building when the wage fund is not yet fixed, labour, from the enterprise-calculation point of view, has a zero or negative price. As a result, enterprises will try to get as high a wage fund as possible in order to create hidden reserves. These can be used to over-fulfil the planned value added by cutting material costs. This pressure from enterprises, due to the incentive system used, will undoubtedly be reflected in methods of production approved by the planners. Then, at the stage of plan fulfilment, the actual performance will tend to deviate from planned tasks because enterprises will have tried to maximize the value added by substituting labour for material means of production within the limits of the approved wage fund. The consequences of this conflict of interest cannot be resolved satisfactorily within the framework of an incentive system based on value added.

B. *What to produce*

Let us now discuss the consequences of value added incentives on what will be produced. The magnitude of value added in 100 zlotys of gross output differs in various branches of production (*e.g.*, it is relatively great in mining and relatively small in the electric power industry) and—what is especially important—it differs also for various products within a given branch of industry or enterprise. For example, the relative share of value added in gross output is greater in the case of handpainted porcelain than for plain porcelain. This fact creates certain problems for economic policy:

1. The difference in the share of value added in 100 zlotys of gross output in various branches of industry makes it necessary to apply bonuses differentiated by branches or, in the case of equal bonuses, to use a properly differentiated turnover tax. These are necessary if we want to avoid unjustified differences in the level of bonuses received by different branches of industry.

2. The different share of value added in various goods makes necessary the use of a turnover tax differentiated by products. Otherwise there will be a tendency to deviate from the planned product-mix.

Hence the properly differentiated turnover tax makes possible the use of price policy as an effective tool for stimulating enterprises to produce in accordance with the tasks prescribed for them in the national plan.

Incentives based on value added do not invalidate the argument put forward in the previous section that, with direct economic calculation, there is a need for a system of two operational prices—one for buyers and one for sellers—due to the external character of the methods of production. Since our discussion of the margin of tolerance existing around every operational price also applies to the incentive system based on value added, we do not have to repeat our previous arguments here.

REFERENCES

[1] W. Leontief, 'Econometrics', *Survey of Contemporary Economics*, Vol. 1, H. S. Ellis, ed., Homewood 1952, pp. 388–411.
[2] K. Marx, *Das Kapital*, Vol. 3 (many editions).
[3] A. Nove, *The Soviet Economy*, New York, 1961.
[4] A. Wakar, ed., *Materialy do studiowania ekonomii politycznej socjalizmu* (Materials for Studying Political Economy of Socialism), Vol. 2, Warsaw, 1962.
[5] —— and J. G. Zielinski, 'Rachunek ekonomiczny bezposredni' (Direct Economic Calculation) *Ekonomista*, Feb. 1961, 61, 17–43.

[6] J. G. Zielinski, *Rachunek ekonomiczny w socjalizmie* (Economic Calculation in a Socialist Economy) (second edition), Warsaw, 1963.
[7] ——, 'An Attempt to Construct a Realistic Theory of Socialist Economy', *Øst-Økonomi*, July 1962, 1, pp. 87–104.

THE ECONOMIC TOOLS
OF PLAN FULFILMENT: II*

The multiplicity of management formulae in a socialist economy. The great number of incentives used in the actual management of socialist economies, requiring the application of a great number of formulae, can all be divided into two large groups: synthetic incentives and specialized incentives. We shall discuss them in turn.

The characteristic feature of synthetic incentives is their universal character. They influence all aspects of enterprise activity in contrast to specialized incentives which influence only selected aspects, *e.g.*, quality, quantity, costs of production and the like.

Thus far, in both the theory and practice of socialist economies, three types of synthetic incentives have been discussed and applied—namely, bonuses based on gross output, profit, and value-added incentive. We do not, however, preclude the invention of other synthetic incentives which are as yet unknown or at least not as yet applied in practice.

Any synthetic incentive can be 'deciphered' differently by different prices and methods of accounting which correspond to it. This means that for every synthetic incentive there exists a group of formulae. The formulae within the group differ mainly in their second and third components. Let us take as an example incentives based on profit and indicate the different formulae which can be used with this class of incentive.

When one applies an incentive system based on total profit, there is the problem that different enterprises have unequal

---

* For further discussion of the problems analysed in this Lecture, see Appendix II.

chances of earning profit, because of their diverse locations, their more or less efficient means of production, variable shifts of demand curve as a result of the appearance of competing products, and variable access to better or worse natural resources.

The substantial differences in the level of profit bonuses in different enterprises can lead to a cumulative process of splitting up all enterprises into efficient and inefficient because of the influx of the best people to enterprises paying higher bonuses. Different solutions to this problem lead to different formulae, all based on total profit. Let me mention just two such proposals.

The most common is the use of accounting prices within a given branch of industry. There is one price for buyers, but different prices for sellers, differentiated for the sake of compensating the 'handicapped' enterprises.

This solution, widely used in extractive industry, is far from ideal. It improves the profit distribution within the branch of industry, but at the same time it leads to misallocation of production. The suggested policy of accounting prices increases the share of high cost producers within the total volume of production at the expense of lower cost producers.

Another proposal [7] for solving the problem of profit distribution within a branch suggests a revaluation of capital from time to time and the use of differentiated rent for the employment of natural resources. This procedure resembles changing the value of capital according to the profitability it renders. Adopting this proposal would lead to different management formula, also based on total profit but with different price and accounting systems.

Still another variant of the formula including incentives based on profit is the proposal to connect bonuses not with total profit but with marginal profit, i.e., the increase of profit over the previous year's level [2, 4]. In this solution the problem of fixed costs disappears, but it is quite complicated in its operational form. We shall not discuss it here: it is just mentioned as an example of yet another formula based on profit.

Let us now turn to a brief discussion of specialized incentives. One of their characteristic features is the frequent absence of prices and cost calculation in their formulae. A bonus based on quality achieved is a good example. In calculating quality bonuses for a multi-product firm, the use of prices is limited to output prices which serve as weights together with 'grade coefficients'.* Cost calculation is totally absent. What interests us here is the fact that in this formula the use of value categories is extremely restricted and this is characteristic of many formulae based on specialized incentives, *e.g.*, economizing certain inputs, introducing technical progress, etc.

As we shall see later on, the fact that specialized incentives formulae are usually constructed without the help of value categories is one of the reasons for their being the most elastic component of the whole management system.

The majority of both economists and planners agree on the superiority of synthetic incentives. Nevertheless, the importance and the wide application of specialized incentives are not diminishing in management practice. For instance, in Poland in 1960 there were close to fifty specialized incentives in use [3]. How can this be explained?

It seems to us that there are three main reasons for this fact.

First of all, some of the so-called 'synthetic' incentives are not, in fact, synthetic. This is especially true for gross output incentives which do not stimulate such factors as cost reduction,

---

* Let us assume that two goods are produced, A and B, and their price ratio is 2:1. Let us assume also that the results for the period under consideration are as follows:

Grade	Grade coefficient	Production of A (in physical units)	Production of B (in physical units)
I	1	10,000	—
II	2	1,000	1,000
III	3	8,000	20,000

If we recalculate these results into units of B (according to the 2:1 price ratio) we have 59,000 accounting units (38,000 of A and 21,000 of B), which when weighted according to grade coefficients give us an average quality slightly below second grade (134,000 : 59,000=2.27). This index of average quality achieved is the basis for the quality bonus. In the case given, the index may be too low for any bonus at all, as there usually is a limit, say of two, above which no bonus is paid.

effective use of labour force, etc. To a lesser extent it also applies to value-added incentives, especially insofar as the use of labour is concerned. Obviously, incentives based on profit are the most universal kind, and with their application there is less need for the supplementary use of specialized incentives. Profit-based incentives, however, still play a minor role in managing socialist economies despite the widespread discussion stressing their merits. Here are the findings of a special commission, created to investigate the role and scope of different 'success indicators' in the Polish economy:

> '... the success indicators based on gross output in constant prices and on commodity production (produkcja towarowa) in current prices inclusive of turnover tax (ceny zbytu), play a major role in planning and controlling the wage fund. All other 'success indicators' are used in only 18 per cent. of the total number of enterprises, which produce altogether 23 per cent. of industrial production. ... The scope of application of gross output and commodity production as a 'success indicator' (nearly 82 per cent. of all enterprises), and their importance (they are the basis for calculating and adjusting the wage fund, a necessary condition for paying bonuses to the managerial staff, and the basis for general evaluation of enterprise performance) makes them *nolens volens* the most important of all success indicators . . .'[5]

The second reason for the widespread use of specialized incentives is the faulty construction of management formulae. This fault may appear in any one of the three components of the formula. The basic incentive itself, as is the case with the gross output, may be a wrong one. But even incentives based on profit may require the supplementary use of specialized incentives if other components of the formula are faulty; for instance, if operational prices are not equilibrium prices, if the use of certain inputs (*e.g.*, capital or land) is not included in cost calculation, etc.

Finally, we have to realize that for many reasons, both practical and doctrinal, the incentive component of the formula is the most elastic one. The regulations existing in Poland do not allow change in prices of producers' goods within the yearly planning period, and the price change for the next year has to be announced at least 3 months in advance. This creates the problem of how to influence the behaviour of managerial staff if the need to change product or input mix arises in the process of fulfilling the yearly plan. With constant prices it cannot be done through the impact of synthetic incentives, so there remains the choice between administrative orders (*e.g.*, forbidding or limiting the use of certain inputs) and using the specialized incentives (*e.g.*, giving special bonuses for economizing certain inputs).

Turning now to the doctrinal reasons, the pragmatic point of view on incentives usually prevails. The same cannot be said about the prices and cost calculation, which have 'to conform to value', so that they can properly measure the socially necessary costs, etc. These considerations frequently prevent them from proving an efficient tool of plan fulfilment. If the existing management formula does not render satisfactory results, the 'easiest' way to remedy this is to introduce the new specialized incentive.

Simple and composite formulae. By a 'simple' formula, we understand a formula which consists of one incentive (*e.g.*, profit), one price system (*e.g.*, average cost-plus pricing), and one method of accounting. By a composite formula we understand a number of simple formulae used simultaneously to direct and stimulate a given economic unit (enterprise, industrial association, etc.) The characteristic feature of a composite formula is that it can always be broken down into a number of simple formulae each consisting of the three components. The composite formula can be defined as a set of simple formulae, either formally interrelated or not.* The former is the case when fulfilling one success indicator is a formal condition for a bonus for another success indicator. For instance, without fulfilling the assortment plan one is not entitled to a bonus for fulfilling the gross output, and the like.

The composite formula usually consists of one or more synthetic incentives (in practice, we know formulae which

---

* In practice, however, the simple formulae used jointly for stimulating a given economic unit are always interrelated and frequently contradictory to each other.

consist of two synthetic incentives, gross output and profit) and a number of specialized incentives. The final effect of the composite formula is the result of the stimulating impact of the many simple formulae with which the composite formula is constructed. When the composite formula has a complicated structure, as is usually the case, owing to the fact that new specialized incentives are introduced in the process of 'improving' the incentives system, it is difficult to predict the final impact of the composite formula on producers' behaviour. It is difficult, if not impossible, to co-ordinate properly different bonuses and their corresponding prices and accounting methods, so that this complex whole will function according to the planners' preferences.

One more difficulty in constructing the composite formulae should be mentioned. As we have pointed out in the previous lecture, to each incentive system there corresponds a certain price system. Planners, however, have at their disposal only two price systems, namely, programming prices and operative prices. Moreover, both of these price systems are based on the same principle, although the levels of some of these prices differ, because the programming prices are the operative prices from a given date. As a result, the same prices must be used with gross output and profit incentives, even though completely different price systems would seem to be necessary for purposes of efficient management.

Another danger in applying complex and mutually competitive incentives can be mentioned. The existence of a complex bonus system leaves enterprises, to an extent limited only by the existence of planned orders, free to choose the incentives most convenient for them and to ignore others. As Professor B. Blass has rightly pointed out, [1] the obligatory character of socialist planning has a different meaning in the process of plan construction and in the process of plan fulfilment. The enterprise *has* to submit a plan in accord with the goals given to it by higher authorities. No other plan would be accepted. This he calls the 'directly obligatory character' of plan construction. In the process of plan fulfilment the enterprise *should* fulfil (or overfulfil) the planned task and is stimulated to do this by a system of bonuses and sanctions. This he calls the 'indirectly obligatory character' of plan fulfilment.

In practice, the system of incentives and sanctions within the composite formula leaves the enterprise an ample field for manoeuvre, and as a result, plan fulfilment frequently deviates seriously from the planned tasks. These deviations are not accidental, but correspond to maximum-bonus product-mix, given the constraints. The Polish Minister of Internal Trade, Dr. M. Lesz, recently quoted a number of examples of not fulfilling the assortment plan and commented: 'We have here certain regularity, certain law: the level of plan fulfilment of a given good is directly proportional to the value of production per hour of labour', and he traced it to the use of gross output as a main success indicator. [6]

The system of stimulating producers through a complex incentive system is nowadays not widely supported either in Poland or in other socialist countries. Some think, however, that this complexity is not the chief cause of the evil and that the system can be improved by changing the nature and ratio of individual incentives only. But is this possible? Our previous practice has been entirely based on these partial improvements, and we have to appraise the results of these improvements negatively.

It does not seem to us that this traditional approach promises great success. The supporters of composite formulae do not appreciate the interdependence of the elements of the incentive system. Can these interdependences be weighted and the most suitable solution selected? Experience gained hitherto would suggest a negative answer.

We are rather critical about a complex incentive system. However, we also see difficulties in applying a synthetic incentive.

First of all, the equilibrium price system is necessary. However, if we think of prices equilibrating a given plan rather than shadow prices which reflect an optimal solution, an equilibrium system seems to be within the range of practical possibility. If planners are able to set approximate equilibrium prices for consumers' goods where demand is more difficult to predict and more unstable, there is no reason why they cannot equally succeed in fixing prices for the means of production.

Secondly, it can also be noted that the operation of the single incentive is, in practice, almost impossible, especially in a planned economy. If the plan consists, as it must, of many indices, one can hardly expect that the higher authorities will disregard them completely in their evaluation of enterprise management, even if formally there are only profit bonuses. If this is the case, the importance the enterprise management will attach to particular plan indices will always, to some extent, reflect their appraisal by higher organs of the economic hierarchy.

It is worthwhile to note these difficulties, because some practical conclusions can be drawn from these possible dangers.

First, profit incentive should be strong enough so that if the question arises as to whether a larger profit should be gained at the expense of not meeting some plan indices, it is resolved in favour of the profit.

Second, the profitability gained should be an essential, and even the only criterion used by higher authorities for appraising the activities of the enterprise. If the Central Planning Board is not satisfied with the material results produced by profit maximization it should introduce the necessary changes in the parameters on which enterprises base their decisions, rather than change the criterion for their appraisal or introduce additional criteria. If there should arise a need for immediate action which cannot be taken through price change, due to the requirement of price stability during the yearly planning period, administrative orders or short-term rationing of producers goods would seem to be a better device than the introduction of specialized incentives. The latter, once introduced, tend to proliferate and make it more difficult to predict both enterprise behaviour and the end result on plan fulfilment of applying a complex, composite formula.

Management formula and the quality of information. For the purpose of planning and management, the Central Planning Board receives from the lower units two types of information:

proposals for planned targets for the next planning period and reports on plan fulfilment.

In many cases, however, both types of information, especially the former, are consciously distorted by the lower units. The extent to which such information is distorted depends to a great extent on the type of management formula used.

In the case of gross output bonuses it is advantageous for the enterprise to underestimate its production possibilities and to report the need for as high a level of inputs as possible. Low plan targets and approved high input norms facilitate the over-fulfilment of plan tasks and bring high bonuses. A formula based on gross output is especially detrimental for the quality of information supplied by the lower units.

Other formulae (*e.g.*, those based on profit or value-added), do not have this negative effect on the quality of information. With a profit bonus, for instance, the enterprise has nothing to gain by not reporting its capacity or requiring higher inputs than needed.*

The above thesis may prove untrue if the changes which are being introduced to the formula can be traced to the information supplied by the enterprise, *e.g.*, if, as a result of reporting increased capacity, the prices are lowered, or if improvements in the quality are entirely passed to the customers. Attempting to avoid these consequences, the lower units will try to withhold information which in the past proved detrimental to their economic interest.

We may note here that the problem of full and true information cannot be solved by the proper choice of management formula alone. The techniques of human relations have also to be used to achieve higher levels of social consciousness and better understanding of the basic unity of individual and social interests in a socialist economy.

The empirical character of the formula. The goals we want to achieve through the management formulae are purely pragmatic; we want to induce management decisions in conformity

---

* Requiring higher inputs as a hidden form of building up reserves may be advantageous with any form of incentive system, if the enterprise expects that there may be difficulties in obtaining them by normal ways.

4

with planned tasks, and we want to improve the general quality of managerial work.

Obviously enough, practical results only should be the basis for judging the efficiency or inefficiency of the formula as a whole and of its constituent elements.

The pragmatic character of the incentives is generally accepted. Everybody understands that we use incentives to get the desired results: increased production, proper product mix, methods of production which we consider optimal, etc.

However, the same is not true for the other two elements of the formula: prices and methods of accounting. Here the pragmatic approach frequently gives way to a dogmatic approach. Many people think that prices should reflect 'value', however defined, irrespective of the type of the formula in operation, and they suppose that there is an 'objectively right' price in every circumstance and for every cost calculation.

In the previous lecture we have tried to prove that the choice of any given incentive system determines the system of operational prices which can be effectively used in conjunction with it and vice versa. Here we may note that the same is true about cost calculation. The proper cost calculations have to be different depending upon whether profit, cost reduction, or gross output is the success indicator. In the case of the first, price changes should be taken into account in cost calculation; in the other two, eliminated from it. [8, 9] The existing practice is that irrespective of the incentive system used (including profit incentive), the effect of price changes on success indicators is carefully eliminated. This is a striking example of disregarding the interrelationships between cost calculation and incentive systems. As a result of this practice, price changes even with profit incentives cannot be used as a tool for influencing managerial decisions. It is not astonishing, therefore, that the higher authorities have to rely on specialized incentives and/or administrative orders to influence the product mix and methods of production.

It may be interesting to note that the pragmatic approach is most limited in respect to formulae based on synthetic incentives: profit, gross output, value added. To a much lesser extent this is true in regard to the second and third components (prices and methods of accounting) of the formulae based on specialized incentives, *e.g.*, quality, economizing raw materials, and the like. The obvious reason for this is the fact that these formulae are constructed without the help of value categories (prices, cost of production), the categories where established ways of thinking are the strongest.

The integral character of the formula. The second conclusion we can draw from our analysis is the integral character of the formula. Incentives, prices, and methods of accounting constitute a unity and should be treated as an interrelated whole in both the theory and the practice of managing socialist economies. Most unfortunately, however, the postulate of formula integrity is not, as a rule, fulfilled. There are frequent attempts to consider and to change incentives, prices, and methods of accounting independently one of another.

Why is the unity of the formula not respected in theory and practice? We see three main reasons for this state of affairs:

(1) Survivals of a dogmatic approach in the theory of prices and cost calculation, which we have already noticed. These prevent many people from seeing that prices and cost accounting may have to be adjusted to a given incentive system. As a result, irrespective of the incentive system used, the same prices and cost accounting method are used, sometimes with very negative results, as is the case with gross output.

(2) Inelasticity of prices because of other functions they fulfil in addition to their being an element in the management formula (for instance, their distributive functions). These functions, however, can be reconciled. But for this it may be necessary to use a system of double pricing and/or the proper policy of turnover tax.

(3) The complexity of composite formulae now in use. Let us recall the fifty specialized incentives presently used by Polish management practice. For a given economic unit between half a dozen and a dozen different bonuses frequently apply. In such a complex system it is very difficult indeed to see and account for all interrelationships and feedbacks existing between different simple formulae and their composite ele-

ments. If there is a change in one of the incentives within the composite formula, this usually is accompanied by appropriate changes in *its* methods of calculation, but, as a rule, we do not adjust to and hardly even see many other interrelationships which exist and should be taken into account. This is one more argument in favour of using simple formulae based on one synthetic incentive, or at least, if composite formulae cannot be avoided, of using a relatively simple composite formula, consisting of only very few supplementary specialized incentives.

The choice of proper formula. All formulae are of empirical character, and to all formulae the requirement of proper coordination of their three basic elements applies. But there are many formulae which can be internally consistent. There may be formulae based on different synthetic incentives: profit, gross output, value added. There may be also internally consistent composite formulae, at least if we leave aside the practical difficulties of their construction. This creates the problem of choosing the proper formula.

It would be an illusion to think that there exists an optimal formula irrespective of the general conditions in which the economic process takes place. For instance, it seems to us that a very tight economic plan requires a different formula from the plan which calls for a slower rate of growth of the economy.* It is not accidental that even the market economies used different methods of directing production under conditions of war economy, when it was necessary to speed up the rate of growth considerably and when structural changes in the economy were to be achieved in a relatively short time.

It is quite probable that not only general conditions have to be taken into account in the choice of proper formula, but also *specific* conditions of different branches of the economy: industry, agriculture, big and small scale enterprises, etc.

It also seems that the different formulae used in the national economy should change over time. The reason for these changes

---

* It is our contention that tight economic plans require centralized management to which correspond non-parametric, two-part formulae, consisting of incentives and methods of accounting only. See Lecture Ten and point three of the next section.

is not only the need for improving their efficiency. The changes should also reflect the changes in the national economy itself: the changing importance of different branches, the new methods of planning and also the higher level of social integration achieved.

The management formula as an analytical tool. The concept of management formula seems to be a useful analytical tool.

(1) Applied in some case studies of Polish enterprise, it helped to clarify the complex mechanism by which our enterprises are managed. By using the concept of a three-part formula and by breaking the composite formula into a number of simple ones, it was easier to picture the existing multi-incentive system and to study the complex interrelationships, both formal and informal, which exist between its different elements.

(2) The concept of the management formula also proved helpful in explaining the nature of price systems in socialist economics. Depending on the type of economic calculation, the prices used in plan construction (programming prices) and the prices for stimulating producers for plan fulfilment (operational prices) can be the same or different. In the practice of socialist economies, they are different. By explaining the operational prices as a part of management formula only, their functions and limited role become clear. The purpose of operational prices, together with cost calculation, is to 'decipher' a given incentive. Their function is to stimulate producers to fulfil the planned tasks, and to simulate the choice already made in the process of plan construction, but they are not the basis for the original choices themselves.

(3) Finally, the concept of the formula was used to clarify our understanding of centralized and decentralized management within the framework of planned, and hence, of centralized socialist economies. We presented this problem as follows: in the case of complete centralization, management is effected with the help of incentives (material and non-material) based on recognition by higher authorities of the enterprise's performance* together with regulations transmitted to the enterprise as to what is to be produced and how. This formula

lacks a parametric part. Prices are here not parameters for choice, but constitute just a component part of the methods of accounting, in the same way as other regulations controlling the operation of enterprises do. The non-parametric formula, consisting of two elements only—incentives and regulations— is consequently a distinctive feature of the centralized management. Conversely, in the case of a distinct division of the formula into the three components of incentives, rules of accounting (regulations) and prices as *parameters*, for the indirect guidance of enterprises, we are dealing with a decentralized management of the economy. This decentralization concerns only the forms of management of the national economy without, however, changing its content, since decisions remain in the hands of the central organ. We may note here that the management formula can have a non-parametric character, irrespective of the type of incentive used. Many people think that the use of profit incentives is tantamount to decentralized management. This does not necessarily have to be the case, if by decentralization we mean, as in our definition, the indirect steering of the economy through changes in parameters which are the basis for managerial decisions at the enterprise (and/or industrial associations) level. For instance, the formula based on profit incentive but with the effects of price changes eliminated from the cost calculation (the type of profit-based formula used in Polish practice) is a non-parametric, and hence a centralized management formula. We shall return to this problem in Lecture Ten. For further discussion of management formulae see also Appendix II.

* By incentives based on recognition we mean bonuses not connected with fulfilment of indices strictly defined and expressed in quantitative terms (as, for example, profit or gross output) but bonuses awarded on the basis of a general evaluation of the enterprise's performance as seen by the higher authorities.

REFERENCES

[1] B. Blass, 'Mierniki oceny dzialalnosci przedsiebiorstwa przemyslowego w gospodarowaniu funduszem plac' ('Success Indicators of Industrial Enterprise and the Wage Fund'), *Konferencja o miernikach oceny dzialalnosci przedsiebiorstwa. Materialy przedkonferencyjne* (Materials for Conference on Success Indicators), Mimeographed n.d.

[2] W. Brus, 'Koncepcja bodzcow opartych na zysku' ('The Concept of Incentives Based on Profit'), *Zycie Gospodarcze*, Nos. 25 and 26, 1957.
[3] B. Fick, 'W sprawie dzialania bodzcow ekonomicznych: uwagi dyskusyjne' ('On Functioning of Economic Incentives: Polemic Remarks'), *Nowe Drogi*, No. 1, 1962.
[4] M. Kalecki, 'Schemat nowego systemu bodzcow i nakazow' ('The Outline of the New System of Incentives and Orders'), *Zycie Gospodarcze*, No. 29, 1957.
[5] Komisja powolana zarzadzeniem nr. 35 Prezesa Rady Ministrow, uchwalq KERM nr 254/63 i 271/63 (Commission created by Prime Minister's Order No. 35 and Orders No. 254/63 and 271/63 of Economic Committee of Ministers), 'Kryteria oceny dzialalnosci przedsiebiorstw przemyslowych' ('Criteria for Evaluating Performance of Industrial Enterprises'), *Konferencja o miernikach oceny dzialalnosci przedsiebiorstwa. Materialy przedkonferencyjne.* (Materials for Conference on Success Indicators). Mimeographed n.d.
[6] M. Lesz, 'Bodzce i mierniki przedsiebiorstwa przemyslowego a potrzeby rynku' ('Incentives and Success Indicators of Industrial Enterprise and Requirements of the Market'), Ibidem.
[7] A. Wakar, *Wybrane zagadnienia ekonomii politycznej socjalizmu* (Selected Problems of Political Economy of Socialism), Warsaw, 1957.
[8] ——, *Morfologia bodzcow* (Morphology of Incentives), Warsaw, 1963.
[9] ——, 'Prices, Incentives, and Calculation Methods', *On Political Economy and Econometrics, Essays in Honor of O. Lange*, Warsaw, 1964.

THE CONSUMPTION MODEL AND THE TOOLS OF ITS IMPLEMENTATION

Consumption planning

1. *Who constructs the consumption model?* Every citizen, depending upon the role he plays in society, represents a different attitude as to what the consumption model should be. In a planned economy it is functionally and institutionally an objective of the Central Planning Board to represent the viewpoint of the entire society on the desirable structure of consumption.

The Central Planning Board cannot refuse to lay down a consumption model and to plan its volume and structure in detail. There are two reasons for this. One is the integrity of the economic plan which cannot be constructed or balanced properly unless the consumption sphere is taken into consideration. Consumption cannot be exempted from concrete and detailed planning. 'General proportions' or 'general directives' which supposedly may be included in a plan and only later detailed when the enterprises implement the plan are as invalid in the sphere of consumers' goods and services as they are in the plan for production of capital goods. This follows from the argument presented in Lecture Four supporting the thesis that operative planning is always concrete and that 'general proportions' are merely the aggregates of concrete quantities into which they may always be divided.

The second justification for laying down an explicit consumption model is that the CPB must have a price and income policy. If the CPB sets out the prices and incomes of the population, this, together with the given consumers' tastes, determines the volume and structure of effective demand. The structure of effective demand then determines the supply of consumer goods necessary for market equilibrium. It is thus impossible to set price and income policy without having a consumption model in mind.

The very fact that the Central Planning Board must set out the consumption model, *i.e.*, must chart the volume and detailed structure of consumption as an integral part of the overall economic plan, does not mean that public opinion has no influence on the way the model is constructed. For it is a functional and institutional objective of the Central Planning Board to represent the viewpoint of the entire society on the desired structure of consumption—*i.e.*, to assume the attitude or point of view which individual citizens would take if they considered the interests of the society as a whole.

Therefore, the fact that the Central Planning Board sets the consumption model need not in itself result in a divergence between the established consumption model and public opinion in this matter. Nor does it imply an insignificant role for consumers in forming the consumption model. Such a divergence would result only if the Central Planning Board disregarded the preferences of consumers both in their role as citizens and as self-interested householders.

2. *The role of the consumer in setting out the consumption model.* A knowledge of consumers' views on the consumption model is essential both when they think in terms of the entire society or in terms of family preferences.

How can we ascertain the views of the consumers in these different respects ? As far as their views in terms of the entire society are concerned, we have to rely on non-market sources of information such as the press (both articles and letters to the editors), radio, all kinds of polling, and other methods of direct research into consumers' opinions. In a society organized in a sufficiently democratic way, the non-market sources automatically convey what consumers think of the existing consumption model and in what way they want it to be changed.

The source of information on the family preferences of consumers is the market place. But the data from the market should always be considered together with the first group of information, particularly when alternative sources of purchase are lacking. For, even if the selling process is smooth, it does not necessarily mean that the consumers are satisfied; sometimes they buy because they have no other choice and often it is not possible to delay the satisfaction of a particular need.

3. *What cannot be learned from demand analysis*. Without denying the significance of demand analysis and of all kinds of demand elasticities for efficient implementation of the consumption plan, we have serious doubts concerning the role attributed to it in setting up this plan and in determining the ways in which it should change.

Demand and needs. The first misunderstanding in this sphere, often found in the literature, is identifying demand analysis with the investigation of consumers' needs. In practice effective demand indicates only one point on the map of consumers' preferences. Moreover, this point we ourselves determined by fixing the price ratios and incomes.

Changes in demand and in the consumption model. Correct interpretation of the information obtained from effective demand is of both theoretical and practical significance. Effective demand which differs from what we had expected indicates only that we appraised consumers' preferences incorrectly.

This does not in any way predetermine how the planners should react to this fact. It merely indicates a contradiction between the consumption model and its means of implementation. Only a concrete analysis of each case will enable the CPB to decide whether the consumption model itself should be changed or whether alternative prices, incomes, and trade margins should be selected for change. The only certain thing is the necessity to react: this is dictated by the pragmatic claim that the consumption plan like any other should be internally consistent. However, whether supply itself or the consumers demand should be changed is not and cannot be determined in advance. This must be decided each time on the basis of concrete analysis.

4. *The consumption model and consumers' sovereignty*. The existence of a consumption model means that in a planned economy 'the consumers' sovereignty' does not exist in the way

traditionally presented in economic literature. There is no automatic relationship between changes in effective demand and the allocation of resources, even in the consumer goods sector. This does not mean that reallocation resulting from changes in effective demand cannot or should not appear under socialism. But there is nothing automatic about it. Effective demand on the market and changes in the consumption plan (reallocation of resources) are connected by means of the planning apparatus. The CPB balances the consumption plan by either changing the plan itself or its means of implementation (*i.e.*, prices, incomes, trade-margins, etc.), or both.

The practical result of the consumption model is that there are two consumer goods price systems in a planned economy: operational prices in the consumer goods sector to guide producers in achieving the consumption plan, and consumer goods prices for consumers in implementing the consumption plan.*

5. *What is the consumption model based on?* Five groups of factors should first of all be considered when the consumption model is being drawn up. Firstly, there are factors which we can loosely term 'biological'. In foodstuffs their influence can be observed most clearly in the form of the so-called rational standards of nutrition, but extends also to a large number of other fields, including the designing of towns, furniture, and places of work. The second group of factors is fashion and taste. The consumption plan is generally a compromise between what is regarded as 'good taste' and the existing habits of some consumers. The third group influencing the form of the consumption model is that of economic factors. Equal use values with respect to number of calories, durability, etc., might, for example, be obtained from various raw materials, making it easier or more difficult to balance the

---

* As we have already pointed out in Lecture Three (Direct Economic Calculation), in a socialist economy we can distinguish three kinds of prices:
(a) 'operational prices', which are used within the socialist sector for stimulating producers—sellers and buyers—to plan fulfilment; (b) 'programming prices' used for construction of the plan, and (c) 'consumers' prices', which have to equalize supply and demand, and at the same time, influence consumption patterns in the socially desirable direction (as seen by the Central Planning Board).

plan. Vegetable and animal fats, natural and synthetic fabrics, etc., could serve as an example here. When setting the consumption model, we should weigh the possibility of substitutions, which allow us to reach the determined indices of consumption (*e.g.*, number of yards of woollen or of other similar materials *per capita*) with less strain on the balanced plan equilibrium. Fourthly, the consumption model must take into consideration the planned income structure. For the significance of income differentiations as an incentive fully appears only when accompanied by a proper variety in the supply of consumer goods. Fifthly, 'the national consumption model' must take into account the existence of social, professional and regional stratification. Thus, *de facto*, we have many consumption models, and the national consumption model is only an aggregate of more detailed ones.

*Implementation of the Consumption Plan**

The implementation of the consumption plan is made up of two elements: fulfilment of the consumption model by the producers of consumer goods, and fulfilment of the consumption model by consumers, *i.e.*, selling out consumer goods produced.

The first problem will not be analysed here since it is theoretically similar to the problem of fulfilling the production plan as a whole. (It does not matter whether these are means of production or consumer goods.) Here we intend to discuss the second problem, *i.e.*, the means by which consumers are guided and induced to fulfil the consumption model.

   1. *Plan-consumer relations: the policy of incomes and prices.* The real incomes of the population are the content of the consumption policy. They are reached by a policy of prices and nominal incomes. We shall deal here with prices only. Of course, this assumes the existence of a definite policy of nominal incomes; for prices and nominal incomes must be established jointly in order to achieve desired real incomes.

* The contents of sections (1) and (3) draw heavily on the article 'Prices in the Direct Economic Calculation' by A. Wakar and J. Beksiqk (*Ekonomista*, No. 5/1962) by permission of the authors.

Prices, operating in connection with money incomes, are a basic tool for realization of the consumption plan. The price ratios and the price-level, and the level of nominal incomes determine whether consumers choose the 'basket' of goods in accordance with the plan. Research into consumers' reactions to these tools, or analysis of market demand, is of great significance for the proper utilization of these methods. In the light of what we said earlier about the present method of planning, the basic aim of this research is not to work out the plan, but to implement it properly.

When consumer goods are distributed through the medium of money, the successful implementation of all consumption plans requires one consistently constructed system of market equilibrium prices. In other words, the planned volume of goods must be distributed to the consumer by means of these prices, leaving neither excess stocks nor unsatisfied demands. Both these deviations from the market equilibrium have unfavourable results. Directly, they signify failure to accomplish certain objectives of the consumption plan; indirectly, they have a destructive influence on the social basis of production, e.g., through the phenomenon of the 'producer's market'.

The ratios of market-prices cannot be accidental (as happens, for example, with reference to programming prices). This follows from the fact that all goods are interrelated by substitution and complementarity. On the other hand, within the framework of free choice, a consumer may shift his demand from certain goods to others as he wishes: among other things this behaviour is directed by the price ratios. Under such conditions one must reckon with the possibility that a partial change in the prices of certain goods will shift demand to other goods. Thus, if these changes are not adjusted to the entire price system and adapted to the present structure of supply of all consumption goods, the equilibrium of the whole market may be disturbed and the planned objectives may not be realized.

The thesis that it would be desirable to base price ratios of consumer goods on the marginal rates of transformation often appears in economic literature.* The authors of this theory accept production conditions as some kind of 'objective' basis for determining the structure of individual consumption. However, the implementation of this theory does not mean that the consumers' behaviour is unilaterally dependent upon production conditions. Within the market system, the transformation ratios themselves would in turn also be determined by consumers' choices. This proposal makes it necessary to adjust mutually the technical conditions of production and the model of individual consumption.†

Even if we assume for the sake of the discussion that we do have at our disposal a price and cost system which correctly reflects the marginal rates of transformation, the question of whether such a solution is proper arises. Technical conditions of production depend upon factors (amongst others, technical progress and scientific development) which do not change in the same way as social preferences about individual consumption. Historically, the production system, seldom conforms to social view on rational consumption.

The concept under discussion is based upon the acceptance of a certain external principle of price fixing, regardless of the concrete conditions of the problem to be solved. If while setting the consumption plan the Central Planning Board determines prices according to such an external principle, then, as a rule, it must face contradictions which make solution of the problem impossible. For the consumption plan in physical quantities would coincide only by accident with the structure of prices, since each of them is based upon a different principle. There is thus no reason why prices based on marginal

---

* *Vide* W. Brus—'Niektore problemy teorii cen w gospodarce socjalistycznej' ('Selected Problems of Price Theory in a Socialist Economy') in *Zagadnienia ekonomii politycznej socjalizmu* (*Problems of Political Economy of Socialism*), Warsaw, 1959, 2nd Edition, particularly chapters II and IV; W. Brus—*Ogolne problemy funkcjonowania gospodarki socjalistycznej* (*General Problems of Functioning of a Socialist Economy*), Warsaw, 1961, p. 258 and others.

† 'From a purely economic point of view, the total coincidence of the equilibrium price system with the properly constructed initial price system indicates the rational allocation of production factors among various alternatives and the proper adjustment of the production structure to the demand structure under given conditions.' (W. Brus, *Selected Problems of Price Theory in a Socialist Economy*, p. 327.)

transformation rates should be equilibrium prices which will fulfil the established consumption plan.

Of course, it would be possible to apply the above-mentioned principle of fixing prices, provided we give up active consumption planning on a national scale. However, since the necessity of implementing social preferences is generally recognized, no adherents of the theory under discussion suggest this. They permit deviations of prices from the ratios determined by the marginal rates of transformation, but only as exceptions to the rule.

We consider even this compromise position wrong. If the necessity of implementing social preferences is recognized (*i.e.*, if an active consumption policy is carried on), then price fixing according to the objectives of this policy should be the rule rather than the exception. Prices should favour the fulfilment of the consumption plan regardless of their relation-ship to the marginal rates of transformation or any other principle.

The theory of fixing prices according to the objectives of the consumption plan does not, in any form, lead to their con-tinuous fluctuation in contrast to the 'stability' of prices when based on the transformation ratios or some other formula external to the consumption plan. Regardless of the formula according to which they are fixed, all prices must be equilibrium prices (*i.e.*, they must react to the changes in the elements making up the equilibrium). The only method of keeping the market equilibrium at a relatively constant price-level is by possessing the proper stocks and reserves (in productive capacity as well as inventories). This is the inevitable cost of having relatively constant market equilibrium prices, and this cost must be paid in every formula of price fixing.

To implement the consumption model more precisely in relation to particular groups of consumers, we apply a policy of (a) variable prices and (b) differentiated prices.

An example of (a) is the variable price of electric power, increasing or decreasing when a certain consumption ceiling has been passed. Sometimes the consumption ceiling itself is flexible, *e.g.*, depending upon the number of electric appliances the consumer owns. The effect of the variable price may be compared with that of an advertisement; it changes the shape of the preference function. With a given average price, the consumer buys less (or more) than when a variable price is in force. [1]

An example of (b) is price discounts, *e.g.*, for cinema, theatre and concert tickets for certain groups of consumers (granted upon proof of membership). They enable certain kinds of consumption to be given preference in relation to certain social groups (*e.g.*, cheap cinema, theatre or concert tickets for students) or influence the consumption model of certain professional or social groups (*e.g.*, cheap train tickets for employees of Ministries and educational institutions). Such effects may also be obtained by a price policy which discriminates in favour of 'standard' as opposed to 'de luxe' models. If the price differential between the two is greater than that warranted by the differences in production cost and use value, the habitual users of 'standard' models get preferential treatment.

2. *The utilization of the trade network for implementing the consumption model: trade margins.* The trade network, whose chief task is to render certain services to consumers, can also be an active tool for implementing the consumption model. But in order to do this principles for adequately fixing and varying trade margins are essential.

The interest of the trade network in the maximization of profit presents trade enterprises with the problem of moulding sales structure to their greatest advantage. Change in the ratio between margins stimulates the trade network to increase turnover in those goods whose margins are increasing, at the expense of the sale of goods whose margins are undergoing a relative decrease. A change in the trade margin may thus prove to be a means of influencing demand as effectively as change in the retail price, and in any case an effective means of supporting the impact of the price change.

However, certain principles of fixing trade margins create incentives which cause the trade network to function in a manner contradictory to the objectives of the consumption model. Fixing the margins as a percentage of the retail prices is one of these principles. It sets in motion counter-incentives for consumers on the one hand and the trade network on the other. For though the increase in the retail price of an item aims at a decrease in consumer demand, the rise in price at the same time means an increase of profit per unit, and this makes the trade network more interested in selling the given goods.

The trade network may also be actively utilized to implement the consumption plan by properly varied bonuses on the volume of turnover.

3. *The tools of influencing the micro-structure of consumption.* Even with the joint manipulation of prices, incomes and trade margins, the planned standards of consumption for different consumers' groups are never fully and precisely realized. This is so firstly because the planning authorities must operate with average quantities. They can successfully implement only average standards of consumption, deviations inevitably appearing amongst certain consumers' groups. This necessitates the application of additional, non-price means of implementing the consumption plan.

Secondly, the general tendency to lower consumers' sensitivity to price changes as real incomes increase moves in the same direction. This dynamic tendency might be observed statically as a difference in the price elasticity of demand in different income groups. As one moves to a higher group, the demand for more and more lines of goods becomes inelastic and price manipulation less effective. A phenomenon which may be called 'wasteful consumption' often arises under these circumstances. By this we mean the behaviour of consumers that is incompatible with social preferences (*e.g.*, the uneconomical use of electric power by consumers with higher incomes).

The application of certain non-price and non-income means for implementing the plan is vital for both the above reasons. Those means aim at directly influencing consumer behaviour. Two extreme categories can be distinguished amongst them. The first of these includes the means which directly diminishes the sphere of free choice by defining which consumer preferences are effective (*i.e.*, which might be the basis of choice). The introduction of a rationing system for certain goods, or the prohibition of the sale of meat or alcohol on certain days can serve as an example of this.* At the other extreme, there are means which do not limit the freedom of choice but mould consumer opinion by persuasive methods so that individual preferences come nearer to social ones. Various forms of propaganda in the field of consumption belong to this category (see below). There is a wide range of intermediate means between these extreme categories.

4. *Influencing consumers' tastes: motivation research, advertisement.* In economic theory preferences, *i.e.*, the tastes and likes of the population, are generally accepted as data. Consumer preferences are presented in the form of so-called indifference curves. The entrepreneur who wishes to increase demand for his goods does not affect the preferences, but only the consumers' choice by influencing the conditions under which the consumers are given the possibility of choice, *i.e.*, primarily by altering the price. With given preferences and hence a given shape of indifference curves, the relative demand for goods A and B depends on the course of the price line, *i.e.*, on the ratio of prices for the goods $A : B$.

In modern market research, consumer preferences are no longer treated as data. Although the theory of economics does not deal with the causes of a given set of indifference curves, market research goes beyond the question of preference and asks: why do consumers prefer goods A to B in a certain ratio, and is it not possible to change this? By consumers' motives we understand all subjective factors (a considerable portion of subjective factors have an objective basis, outside the individual) which determine preferences, and hence, the shape of the indifference curves. Knowledge of the motives behind consumer behaviour broadens remarkably the scope of our ability to influence their acts of choice since it enables us to influence their preferences effectively by (a) properly constructed change in the conditions under which the consumers are given alternatives for choice (*e.g.*, if we realize that the chief reason consumers dislike buying item A is its colour, taste or shape, we must not manipulate the price only) and (b) by a purely mental influence on their attitude towards

* An excessively wide application of these means is not desirable since it affects the social basis of production unfavourably.

certain goods without changing the material conditions on which alternatives are offered to consumers (*i.e.*, the physical aspects of an item, its price and conditions of sale). [2]

There is no reason for a Central Planning Board to remain passive regarding existing consumer preferences. On the contrary, means for actively moulding consumers' tastes in socially or economically desirable directions should be among the tools for implementing the consumption plan. Both motivation research as a tool for finding out the motives behind consumer behaviour on the market and advertising as a method of changing this behaviour, must play an important role here.

Methods of improvement
1. *The present unsatisfactory utilization of the consumption fund.* Few statements are more generally agreed upon than the thesis that the utilization of our present consumption fund is highly unsatisfactory. Moreover, this dissatisfaction is not confined to consumers only. It is also fully shared by the planning bodies, both at the central and at lower levels.

Although it is generally recognized that this state of affairs is unsatisfactory, opinion differs remarkably as to its causes.

2. *Causes.* It is widely believed that faulty utilization of consumption funds stems from inadequate knowledge of consumers' tastes and needs, causing our consumption plan to be set out badly. As a result, the supply of consumers' goods determined by this deficient plan does not conform to the structure of effective demand. This diagnosis obviously points to ways of remedying the situation. Analysis of effective demand and consumers' tastes should correct the consumption plan radically and thus remove the main sources of the present defects.

It is our view that the actual causes of the unsatisfactory situation on the consumers' goods market lie elsewhere; not in a lack of knowledge of consumers' needs or, in other words, in an inability to determine the consumption plan itself, but in the conditions for producer-implementation of the accepted consumption plan. Such conditions, in turn, also affect the shape of the plan itself. Of course, we do not deny the significance of demand analysis (vide: Section I of this chapter) but we consider its main role, as fixing the proper means for consumer implementation of the plan and controlling the effectiveness of these means. We do not think that this analysis is very important in fundamentally improving the material contents of the consumption plan itself. For example, in a number of industrial design exhibitions we have heard positive consumers' opinions concerning particular exhibits. We know then, what the consumers actually want and nevertheless we wait for years before production begins. The causes of the trouble are, then, deeper than simple ignorance of the consumers' wants.

There are general and specific causes for defects in the consumers' goods market.

The main general cause is economic plans which are 'too tight', *i.e.*, which do not provide adequate reserves to meet unforeseen pressures. This may result from poor planning (*e.g.*, a false estimate of the increase in labour productivity), from independent factors causing tension in the originally balanced plan, or from a conscious policy of setting overly high targets, the so-called 'mobilizing tasks' which are designed to squeeze out the maximum output from the economy. Whatever the causes, the results of overly tight plans are always the same: (a) unplanned changes in the consumption model itself, which bring it below original standards; (b) harm to the main tools of consumption plan implementation for consumers as well as producers. Overstrained plans in relation to consumers lead as a rule to an inflationary situation in which the Central Planning Board begins to lose control over prices and incomes; in relation to producers, they minimize the effectiveness of all tools for stimulating producers to implement properly the consumption plan—by assortment as well as quality.

More specific causes are the application of improper management formulae to the consumer goods sector and trade, and misuse by planners of the tools by which consumers are stimulated to follow the consumption model. (These tools were discussed briefly in the previous section.)

The selection of proper management formulae must meet two requirements. First, they must fit general economic conditions in the given period; *e.g.*, as a rule tight plans reduce the effectiveness of the parametric formulae and require instead administrative forms of management. Second, the formulae cannot be internally contradictory, encouraging producers to act contrary to the plan. Unfortunately, the existing management formulae of both industry and trade do not generally meet these requirements.

A defective formula results, first of all, in failure to fulfil the accepted consumption plan particularly in the indices of assortment, patterns, sizes, colouring, etc. Our daily and weekly press unfortunately supplies many examples of not meeting vital consumption plan indices. The defective formula also influences the shape of the plan itself. The consumption plan like any other, is made in collaboration with the entire planning apparatus—from a single enterprise to the Planning Commission. The accepted formula determines the attitude of the enterprise management at its construction as well as implementation stage. To varying degrees, it encourages them to plan contrary to social preferences in this sphere. Even here, the enterprise management, as co-author of the plan, is as a rule aware of consumers' or planners' wants; but in constructing the plan it is stimulated by the existing formula to exert influence in accordance with its economic interest.

The above applies equally to trade management formulae. These formulae fulfil two objectives. Primarily, they implement the trade services model* (which is a part of the consumption plan); and secondly, they aim at using trade as well as other

---

* By the 'trade services model' we mean the standard of services which the trade network has to provide for consumers. The CPB decides what level of services is to be provided, in the form of sales personnel, overheads, full assortment, etc. The trade management formula is then designed with a double task: first, to prevent the trade network from skimping on the prescribed standards of service; and second, to induce the sales personnel to cater to the wishes of the customer. The first task is accomplished by directives communicating the required norms to the trade organizations; the second, by a properly designed incentive system. In the terminology which will be introduced in the following lecture, the first task is accomplished by the 'non-parametric' and the second by the 'parametric' part of the management formula.

means of influencing consumers to implement the material part of the existing consumption plan.

As far as the proper implementation of the consumption plan by consumers is concerned, we have presented our point of view in the previous section. The chief objection against existing practice in this sphere is a lack of co-ordination between the plan (or, in consequence, actual supply) and the means for implementing it.

(a) In the sphere of consumer goods, the principle of 'the price that clears the market' is still not generally accepted and applied. However, 'if supply is determined in the plan and consumer preferences are given, then the application of any price formula except the principle of "the price that clears the market" must lead to material losses. A number of goods are not sold at all and are deteriorating, the cost of storage increases, etc. Fear of financial loss preventing the use of "the price that clears the market" and resulting in material losses, seems to be a remnant of "the money fetishism" in socialist economy.' [3]

(b) In the sphere of shaping the consumers' tastes, it should be stressed that we do not supply consumers' goods according to what we ourselves suggest as fashionable and modern. Illustrated weeklies, and even industrial design exhibitions or fashion shows, launch designs and products vainly sought by consumers on the market at a later date.

We must also remember that we are dealing with a situation in which not only the consumption model but also various other channels influence consumers' tastes.* In most cases, these influences are quite independent of the consumption model but, nevertheless, they actively influence consumers' tastes and thus force us to consider certain accomplished facts when setting up the model itself, as well as when implementing it.

(c) Finally, applied trade margins generally contradict the objectives of existing price policy.

---

* We present a film for its high artistic or socio-political values; but the fact that, for example, the heroes of the film wear narrow trousers does influence consumers' tastes and demand.

Although the improvement of management formulae in the consumer goods sector would facilitate the construction of a better consumption plan and its proper implementation by the producers of goods and services, improvements in the above-mentioned spheres (a, b, and c) are also indispensable for the consumers' smooth implementation of the consumption model without the material losses and social tensions inevitably accompanying disturbances on the consumers' goods market.

REFERENCES

[1] Aleksy Wakar, 'Problem ceny zmiennej' ('The Problem of a Variable Price'), Central School of Commerce, Warsaw, 1936.

[2] Janusz G. Zielinski, *Big business, Z problematyki nowych technik zarzadzania* (*Big Business, The Problems of New Management Techniques*), Warsaw 1962, pp. 173–4, footnote.

[3] Janusz G. Zielinski, *Rachunek ekonomiczny w socjalizmie* (Economic Calculation in Socialism), 2-ed. Edition, Warsaw 1963, p. 163, footnotes.

CENTRALIZATION AND DECEN-TRALIZATION OF DECISION-MAKING

The problem of centralization and decentralization of the process of decision-making has for a long time played a funda-mental role in writings on the theory of the functioning of the socialist economy. As an example we may point to the Polish discussion in the years 1956–8 on economic models, or to the books by W. Brus and C. Bettelheim, [1] [2] which treat the centralization or decentralization of decisions as the basic criterion distinguishing various models of the socialist economy. It is therefore worthwhile to examine this problem in detail, especially since the notions on centralization and decentraliza-tion, although generally based on accepted practice, have their social-political aspects also, and the discussion concerning them is not devoid of emotional elements. At the same time this discussion is marked by a great lack of precision and of defini-tion of even the most fundamental concepts, with the result that decentralization generally means different things to different people. Acknowledging these difficulties, we attempt never-theless to throw some light on the problem.

1. *The concept of decentralization*
Let us begin by defining the pure centralized and the pure decentralized model. The pure centralized model implies (a) that there exist more than one level of organization, and (b) that decisions are made only by the highest level, the central authority. No decisions are made at lower levels [4, pp. 2–3]. The pure decentralized model is a single-level model—it operates without any central authority and implies the exist-ence of more than one centre of decision-making [4, p. 14]

[5 pp. 2–3, 18]. The classic example of a fully decentralized model is the free-competition market.

We shall in this lecture confine ourselves to discussing aspects of centralization and decentralization of the process of decision-making only in connection with the implementation of the plan. In the construction of the plan we assume centralized decision-making.*

We may examine the degree of decentralization of decisions (the delegation of authority) by analysing the management formula of the social economy. By this formula we mean the prices, the methods of accounting, and the incentives considered as a whole, and we use it as a tool of analysis.

Of these three elements—prices, methods of accounting and incentives—we start with the first two. To generalize these, we may replace the word 'prices' by the term 'parameters' which covers, apart from the prices of the means of production, such variables as the rate of interest, rent, and rates of depreciation; 'methods of accounting' we may replace by the term 'statutes', which represents the nonparametric part of the formula, *i.e.*, the set of directives which regulate the activity of a given level within a given organizational structure of the national economy (*e.g.*, enterprises or industrial associations). With the help of these terms we may define the centralization and decentralization of management in the following way:

> by complete decentralization of management we mean the case where the apparatus which implements the plan (at levels other than the central authority) is directed solely by means of parameters;

> by complete centralization of management we mean the case where the apparatus which implements the plan is directed solely by means of the non-parametric part of the formula, the statutes;

> the greater the role of the nonparametric part of the formula in operative management, the greater is the degree of centralization of decisions and similarly for the parametric part of the formula and decentralization.

* Let me also state explicitly that we confine our discussion to the relations between units of a given organizational structure and do not analyse the character of management within these units.

In complete decentralization, the nonparametric part of the formula (*i.e.*, the whole set of directives regulating the activity of a given level) is constant from the point of view of operative management.* Plan fulfilment is governed solely by changes in the magnitudes of the parameters (prices, rent, rates of depreciation, etc.). In complete centralization the nonparametric part of the formula is variable. The statutes are always varied according to the needs of operative management (*e.g.*, it may be directed that the utilization of copper be reduced by a definite amount, that modern construction methods be used instead of traditional, etc.). The parameters are here generally frozen and the corresponding magnitudes lose their parametric character; they cease to play the role of instruments of operative management of the economy and begin to fulfil different functions: prices, for example, become tools of aggregation. In this way the decentralization of decisions means management via manipulation of parameters and centralization, management via directives. Mixed solutions occur in the operative management of the social economy when changes take place both in the magnitude of the parameters and in the nonparametric part of the formula. The degree of centralization or decentralization of management depends upon the role played in operative management by these parameters and directives.

2. *Double and triple-component formulae*

In the fully centralized model the formula in fact has two elements only: the methods of accounting (the nonparametric part of the formula) and incentives based on recognition.† The directives binding upon the enterprise are continually being reformulated (*e.g.*, on one occasion they may include a ban on the use of bricks other than silicate bricks, and another time they may not), and the enterprise is rewarded on the basis of

* Obviously, the statutes also change over time, but in a decentralized structure these changes are introduced not to alter everyday decisions but to change the rules of the game itself.
† By incentives based on recognition we mean bonuses not connected with the fulfilment of indices strictly defined and expressed in quantitative terms (as, for example, profit or gross output), but bonuses awarded on the basis of a general evaluation of the enterprise's performance as seen by a higher authority.

how it has implemented these directives. The rewards constitute incentives based on recognition, since the degree to which the enterprise fulfils its directives cannot be quantified, and it is the central authority which must recognize and evaluate the enterprise's performance of its tasks.

To the decentralized model there corresponds a triple-component formula: prices (parameters), methods of accounting (the nonparametric part of the formula), and incentives. The model is pure when the methods of accounting are kept constant and the operative management is effected exclusively by changing the level of parameters. This, in turn, influences incentives and, therefore, enterprise behaviours.

To various degrees of decentralization of decisions, on the other hand, there correspond various 'mixed' formulae, *i.e.*, formulae where operative management is effected both by parameters and administrative orders.

3. *The problem of multi-unit, multi-level structures*
Thus far, we have analysed the degree of centralization with regard to a single unit. However, when organization involves many units, and possibly many levels as well, the problem becomes more complicated. The degree of decentralization of decisions may be different at different levels. For example, industrial associations may be managed solely by means of parameters, and the enterprises within these associations solely by directives, or vice versa.

Organizational structures may also be found where industrial associations are managed by means of parameters, and within different associations there are different methods of directing the enterprises—in some associations decentralized, in others centralized. An example of just such an organization is the American concern 'General Motors'.* In all these cases we have several different formulae alongside each other, each of which applies to a particular unit. To be able to classify these

* In General Motors, described by Peter Drucker ([3], pp. 40–73) as an example of decentralized organization, decentralization refers to the relations between the board of directors of General Motors as a whole and its thirty divisions, with the proviso that it is the management of the division which defines the form of organization within that division.

models in terms of the formulated definition of centralization or decentralization, we must assess the scope in the organizational structure as a whole of management by means of the parametric or nonparametric parts of the formula. From this it is apparent that the wider the scope of management by means of parameters, the greater the degree of decentralization of decisions and vice versa. This approach proves to be consistent with the analysis of the degree of decentralization of decisions based on the role of horizontal links, which is the subject of the next section.

It must be admitted, however, that our definition of the degree of decentralization of multi-unit structures is not sufficiently precise to enable us to evaluate every possible case without value judgements. For example, let us consider a four-level structure (with a central planning organ, ministries, industrial associations, and enterprises), in which the associations as well as the enterprises are managed by means of parameters. Such a structure may without hesitation be defined in full conformity with our definition of decentralization as being more decentralized than a structure in which only one of the levels (*e.g.*, the enterprises) is managed parametrically. At the same time, however, we would be inclined to classify an organizational structure in which only the enterprises are parametrically managed as being more decentralized than a structure where only the industrial associations are managed by parameters and all other levels—higher and lower—by directives. However, arguments in support of such a view must go further than the formal framework of our definition.

4. *Vertical and Horizontal links*

Let us begin by examining an organizational structure in which there appear only vertical links. Such a structure '. . . may be represented with the aid of the graph known as the dendrite, reminiscent of a branched tree' [4, p. 1]. (See next page.)

Theoretically, it might be possible to imagine that such an organization also can be decentralized according to our definition (*i.e.*, managed exclusively by parameters). However, the lack of horizontal links would mean that the contracts between units on the same level can be made only through a higher level. To accomplish this under conditions of parametric management, different parameters would have to be used for each organizational unit and this would require as many parametrical systems as the total number of units on all the levels.

Diagram 3

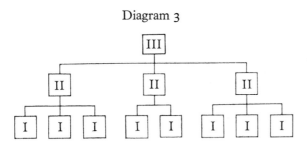

But this situation is obviously not very realistic. Thus in practice the organizational structure in the case where there exist only vertical links is a fully centralized structure, *i.e.*, one which is managed solely by the nonparametric part of the formula.*

To the extent to which the higher level applies the same parameters to many (or all) subordinate units, it fills a role purely of transmission, to use Professor Lange's terminology, and thus serves merely as a clearing house for the transactions between lower units. In effect, therefore, when identical parameters are used the subordinate units are connected horizontally, since the carrying out of transactions through the higher level is in this case of only technical significance.

Let us now turn to an organizational structure in which there appear only horizontal links. It has by definition only one level and is linked up solely by means of parameters. (Use

* Professor Lange in his paper quoted above [4], to which we are greatly indebted, examines the problem of the decentralization of decisions on the assumption that there exist only vertical links. It seems to us, however, that with the complete lack of horizontal links, decentralization of decisions is not in fact possible, or else is limited to the internal affairs of the enterprise, for which contact with other economic units is not necessary.

of the word 'managed' instead of 'linked up' to describe such a structure would here be unsuitable, since management implies the existence of more than one level.) This therefore conforms to our definition of a fully decentralized structure.

But we are concerned here with structures of more than one level, but of various degrees of centralization and decentralization. The notion of vertical and horizontal links makes possible a second scale for measuring the degree of decentralization of decisions, namely, one corresponding to the number of horizontal links, *i.e.*, the numbers of organizational units with which any one of them can enter into direct contact. The fewer the horizontal links, the more centralized the organization is. This scale for measuring decentralization shows a high degree of correlation with our first scale based on the role of the parametric and nonparametric parts of the formula in the management of the national economy. These definitions are almost equivalent. They are not, however, completely equivalent because of the possible appearance of more than one set of parameters, *e.g.*, of separate prices for buyers and sellers. In this case we could have management solely by means of parameters (the decentralized system according to the first scale) without, however, having horizontal links between buyers and sellers (a system not fully decentralized according to the second scale). The definitions of the degree of decentralization as measured by the first and second scales are equivalent only with the condition that there appear just one set of parameters. Without the introduction of this condition, these definitions show only a high degree of correlation.

5. *The economic implications of decentralization of decisions*

The main advantages of decentralization, including the purely economic advantages, undoubtedly lie in its social consequences. The decentralization of decisions favours social integration in production, raises the quality of the labour factor and especially of the managerial staff, thereby increasing economic efficiency. If, however, we ignore this aspect of decentralization, that is, if we ignore the direct and indirect results of its influence on the process of social integration in production, what are its remaining economic implications? In this narrowly economic aspect, the implications of decentralization of decision-making derive solely from the power of those units which implement the plan to make decisions in their own field of activity. This sphere is defined by their statutes. As we have already shown, those statutes are constant from the point of view of operative management and vary only when improvements are made in the methods of planning and management.

The advantages of decentralization are here due to the shortening of information routes. This may have the following results: (a) the speeding-up of the process of decision-making; (b) the avoiding '... of changes in information during its passage between the lower units and the central authority in the case of both reports and directives' [4, p. 7]; (c) the avoiding of costs associated with the transmission and processing of information and with large dimensions of the central planning organ. These problems are well-known and there is no need to discuss them here [4, passim].

Decentralization may have disadvantages, in that erroneous decisions may be made by the lower units (*i.e.*, erroneous from the point of view of the central authority). The main cause of such decisions in a decentralized structure is defective parameters, *i.e.*, parameters which do not lead the apparatus implementing the plan to act according to the preferences of the central authority. This poses the question of the economic conditions necessary for decentralization. Professor Oskar Lange has formulated it in the following way, with which we fully agree:

> the condition whereby decentralization is possible ... or the condition of the automation of management is the possibility of constructing in the lower units such a system of subordinate targets for these units and of incentives resulting in the pursuit of these targets, that the result of the independent activity of the lower units conforms to the targets of the central authority. Simply speaking, the idea is that the lower units should by themselves act in the way in which, in a strictly centralized system, they would be directed to by the central authority. [4, p. 4].

It is evidently very difficult to fulfil the conditions necessary for complete decentralization, *i.e.*, management solely by parameters. In fact, this is so difficult that some economists, such as Wlodzimierz Brus, consider that management solely by parameters is altogether unattainable in a socialist economy.*

Without prejudging the question as to whether a model of the socialist economy managed solely by parameters is possible in practice or not, it is undoubtedly true that one should not make a fetish of either the centralized or decentralized solution. The choice of one or the other must always be determined by whether the conditions for the decentralization of decisions exist and, in connection with this, its relative advantages and disadvantages. It must be remembered that in weighing those advantages, allowance must always be made for the social consequences of decentralization, both direct and indirect, which are not analyzed here.

6. *Direct economic calculation*

a. *Theoretical possibilities.* In our article 'Direct Economic Calculation' [7, p. 19], we put forward the following thesis:

> Between the types of economic calculation and the forms of management of the economy, there exists a definite dependency. For example, in direct economic calculation the only adequate form of management is the use of administrative directives. Market-type calculation, on the other hand, is universal as regards the forms of management to which it is suited. It is especially suited to the use of market parameters as forms of transmitting the planned targets, although it may also be effectively applied in a system of administrative directives.

---

* W. Brus puts forward the following points: (a) Subjective factors. 'The fact is simply that the market mechanism requires a very high degree of precision, of precise correlation of both the type of instrument applied and the quantitative solutions used, with the targets in view. . . . If, therefore, we are not in a position to construct sufficiently precise instruments which act upon the enterprise's decisions in conformity with the plan, decisions must be taken directly and transmitted downwards to the lower units by administrative methods.' (b) Special economic conditions, *i.e.*, '. . . the need to effect profound changes in the economic structure during a comparatively short period of time.' (c) Certain essential features of the socialist economy, namely 'a weak buyer's market' both for producer and consumer goods. The result of all this, the author maintains, is that '. . . every model of the system of operation of the socialist economy should allow for the necessity of applying administrative means to a certain degree' [2, pp. 330, 335].

Formerly, the thesis that in direct economic calculation the transmission of planning tasks must be carried out by administrative directives was supported by us in the following way [9, pp. 122–127]: the kind of economic calculation adopted in drawing up the plan determines the possible forms of transmitting the tasks to the enterprises.

In market-type calculation, calculation is made from the beginning by the enterprise, assumptions being made by the central authority as to the reaction of the enterprise to the given parameters. Here the tools of plan construction (prices, wages, the rate of interest) have been used in achieving economic equilibrium, and hence may simultaneously be methods of transmitting the planning tasks to the enterprises. In this type of calculation prices correspond to the conditions of equilibrium and more or less reflect the marginal rates of transformation in the national economy.

Direct economic calculation, on the other hand, seems to be logically connected above all with that form of management which uses administrative directives and not market parameters. This type of calculation requires that the plan be not only constructed in detail but also transmitted downwards in detail, since the tools of plan construction cannot themselves play the role of parameters which would enable enterprises to take decisions in conformity with the plan. The need to produce a quantity Y of machine X is a function of the whole complex of interrelationships in the national economy as expressed in the input-output table by the central or other planning organs, but invisible to the enterprises and not as a rule reflected with the necessary precision in the system of prices and costs within which the enterprises operate. In the construction of the plan, prices were not used as a tool for plan equilibrium, but served above all for the aggregation of physical magnitudes. In conditions where the prices adopted in the construction of the plan do not correspond to the conditions necessary for equilibrium, it would not be justifiable to use them as alternatives of choice for the enterprises. In drawing up the plan, then, it must be assumed that enterprises will simply carry out the planning tasks. In its construction of the plan, the central

5

planning organ is guided directly by the criterion of physical co-ordination of the plan (so that, for example, the production of steel should correspond to the supply and demand for it); that is, it is guided by the criterion of the internal consistency of the plan and its maximization in the sense of reaching the society's production-possibility curve based on the existing resources, assumed production methods and desired net products.

The simultaneous use of this type of calculation and the principle of transmitting the planning tasks downwards by means of market parameters leads as a rule to undesirable results (it causes a disturbance in the equilibrium of the plan), since prices have not been used as a tool in the plan's construction. In these conditions there arises the problem as to whether, in applying direct economic calculation, we can determine the parameters according to which enterprises would make a choice conforming in its general direction to the plan's targets. Our answer in the past has been that we do not see any such parameters. At present, however, we consider that theoretically speaking such a possibility does exist: namely, although the tools of the plan construction in direct economic calculation are not suitable for making enterprises fulfil the plan, a system of operational prices may be formed which would act as parameters in the prices-accounting methods-incentives formula. This formula would lead enterprises—buyers and sellers—to the fulfilment of the planned tasks as to how and what to produce. These problems were developed more fully in Lectures Seven and Eight.

b. *Decentralization as a result of improvement in direct economic calculation.* The development of the idea of operational prices functioning within the prices-accounting methods-incentives formula has led us to the conclusion that decentralization could be a logical result of the improvement of the direct economic calculation. The reason for this is that the improvement of the direct economic calculation—that is, the improvement both of the plan construction (the attaining of internal consistency of the plan) and of the tools for its fulfilment, *i.e.*, the formula—is a step towards the achievement of the economic conditions necessary for decentralization. From the moment when the plan is not unduly strained and is internally consistent, the improvement of the individual interrelated components of the formula means nothing other than '. . . the construction in the lower units of such a system of subordinate targets for these units, and of incentives resulting in the pursuit of these targets, so that the result of the independent activity of the lower units conforms to the targets of the central authority.' [4, p. 4] The nearer we are to fulfilling these conditions, the more weighted in favour of decentralized solutions is the balance of advantages and disadvantages of the above-discussed decentralization. In this situation, assuming a favourable social climate, the improvement of the direct economic calculation can lead to the decentralization of decisions, *i.e.*, to an enlargement of the role of horizontal links, or in other words the role of the parametric part of the formula. Decentralization may be achieved gradually, as the formula is improved.

Between complete decentralization (management solely by parameters) and full centralization (management solely by directives), there exists a whole gamut of intermediate solutions. Thus, with the existence of a consistent programme for the improvement of the direct economic calculation, there also exists the possibility, as a result of this improvement, of moving to an increasingly decentralized structure. To avoid misunderstanding it must be added that the connexion between the improvement of direct economic calculation and decentralization is not a necessary functional connexion. The improvement of direct economic calculation is a necessary but not sufficient condition for decentralization, since without social demand for decentralization, improvements in the economic calculation will merely denote more effective centralized management.

7. *Centralization and decentralization and the construction of an optimal plan*
In our discussion so far, the problem of the centralization or decentralization of decisions has referred only to the methods

of the organization of plan fulfilment. This has been linked to the construction of the plan only indirectly, by the influence of decentralization on the quality of the labour factor, and consequently on the possibility of establishing higher indices in the plan. However, in the history of the problem of economic calculation in the socialist economy, the centralization and decentralization of decisions has been connected above all with the problem of the construction of an optimal plan. The decentralized solution (the model of Lange) was used as a mechanism to verify the terms on which alternatives for solving the economic problem were offered.

Such verification, however, does not arise in the direct economic calculation, where the correctness of the formula, and hence of its parametric part too, refers to the plan, and is not used to verify its optimality. Operational prices are correct if their functioning within the formula leads to a situation where '. . . the result of the independent activity of the lower units conforms to the plan.' [4, p. 4]

REFERENCES

[1] C. Bettelheim, *Studies in the Theory of Planning*, London, 1959.
[2] W. Brus, *Ogolne problemy funkcjonowania gospodarki socjalistycznej* (*General Problems of the Functioning of the Socialist Economy*), Warsaw, 1961.
[3] P. Drucker, *Concept of the Corporation*, Boston, 1960.
[4] O. Lange, *Niektore zagadnienia centralizacji i decentralizacji w zarzadzaniu* (*Some Problems of Centralization and Decentralization in Management*), Warsaw, 1962.
[5] J. Tinbergen, *Centralization and Decentralization in Economic Policy*, Amsterdam, 1954.
[6] A. Wakar and J. G. Zielinski, 'Socialist Operational Price Systems', *Am. Econ. Rev.*, March 1963, 53, 109–27.
[7] A. Wakar and J. G. Zielinski, 'Rachunek ekonomiczny bezposredni' ('Direct Economic Calculation'), *Ekonomista*, Feb. 1961, 61, 17–43.

[8] J. G. Zielinski, 'An Attempt to Construct a Realistic Theory of Socialist Economy', *Øst-Økonomi*, July 1962, 2, 87–104.

[9] J. G. Zielinski, *Rachunek ekonomiczny w socjalizmie* (*Economic Calculation in a Socialist Economy*, Warsaw, 1963 (second edition).

ARE THERE LAWS OF PLANNING? SOCIALIST PLANNING AND ITS RELEVANCE TO MIXED ECONOMIES

Under this title which I borrowed from Professor L. J. Zimmerman's article 'Are there Laws of Progress?' [9] I want to examine the following problem: are there principles of efficient planning general enough to be valid in any country engaged in national economic planning, irrespective of vast differences in socio-political setting and in level of economic development attained? My answer to this question is 'yes'. Moreover, it seems to me that some of these principles should be spelled out in spite of their very general character because even these most general rules are frequently neglected or violated in the planning practice of many countries. In the second part of my lecture I want to examine briefly the applicability of socialist planning to under-developed countries.

1. *The general principles of efficient planning*
First observation: There is a certain critical size and composition of the public sector, below which effective planning is impossible.

The 'critical size' of the public sector necessary for effective planning is usually defined as a requirement of concentrating in the government's hands so-called 'commanding heights' of the economy. In a recent article Professor V. B. Singh of India formulates this requirement as follows: 'The history of planned economic development reveals that planning cannot be successful unless and until the "commanding heights" (that is, basic industries, transport, communications, banking and finance) are in the public hands.' [6, pp. 54–55]

He argues that an essential feature of the planned economies has been that the national plans have represented binding directives on the government: those who implement them are rewarded and those who violate them punished. Such legal enforcement becomes meaningful only when the scope of the public sector is wide and fully capable of exercising a decisive impact on the movement of the economy. In other words, without drawing the 'commanding heights' into the public sector, it is not possible to shape the destiny of an economy. The author refers to the Indian experience and writes: 'For the private entrepreneurs treat the state directives, as in India, as so many pious wishes of the national leaders and follow their own line—the maximization of profit.'

The British economist and economic historian, Professor A. H. Hanson, an expert on public enterprises and their role in economic development, expressed the same idea with admirable brevity: 'Public enterprise without a plan can achieve something; a plan without public enterprise is likely to remain on paper.' [1, p. 183]

There is still need to stress this functional relationship between the public sector and effective planning, because it is not as yet universally recognized. For example, Professor Benjamin Higgins in his widely read text-book on economic development asserts: 'The need for a plan has nothing to do with the relative importance of the public and private sectors; intervention to alter the decisions of private entrepreneurs is still a plan.' [2, p. 454]

It took time before the thesis that planning is necessary for economic development of underdeveloped countries gained almost universal acceptance, even by the United States government. Until the same is true about the role of the public sector in planning, it is worthwhile to stress the following:

Conclusion: If a developing country wants to engage in effective economic planning its public sector has to embrace certain strategic spheres of economic activity. Otherwise there is a serious danger that its planning remain mainly on paper.*

Second observation: The planning mechanism of any country interested in effective planning has to consist of all the following three elements:

> (1) perspective planning; (2) operative planning; (3) tools of plan fulfilment: (a) for producers and (b) for consumers.

A general picture of the planning mechanism can be presented in a summary fashion with the help of the diagram (see next page).

Differences in the planning mechanism in various countries must exist by virtue of the character of plans (especially short-term plans) and the character of the tools of plan fulfilment, but any planning mechanism which does not consist of the above-mentioned elements is doomed to be ineffective.

Even a cursory look at the planning mechanism in developing countries reveals that there is a serious imbalance between the level of development of perspective planning and all other elements of the planning mechanism.

Most developing countries have some sort of long- or medium-range plan, of better or worse quality, but at the same time both operative plans and tools of plan fulfilment are either in a completely embrionic stage or non-existent. Both current government budgets and economic policies pursued are usually very loosely—if at all—linked with the plan targets, and gross inadequacy exists between planned goals (usually ambitious) and the means of their implementation (usually mild).

It must be obvious that the construction of a perspective plan can in itself have only a very limited beneficial effect on national economy. The possible benefits are:

* The needs for an extensive public sector in developing countries go much beyond its being a requirement for effective planning. In addition, the public sector can be used (1) to increase the overall saving ratio in the national economy, (2) to enter fields which, however important for economic growth, are neglected by private investors, and (3) to accomplish certain economic and social reforms, from breaking the monopoly power of foreign or domestic capital groups to providing cheap housing for low-income strata. (For a fuller discussion of this problem see [5], chap. 5.)

Diagram 4

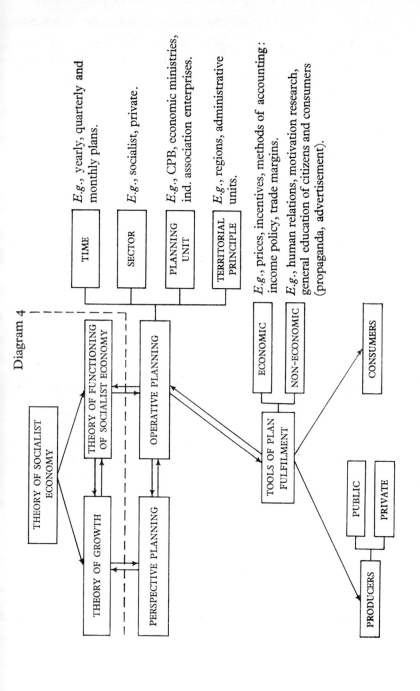

making the country eligible for receiving foreign aid,

improving the knowledge about the economy, as the plan construction is usually accompanied by a more or less intensive 'fact finding' campaign which includes a demographic census, industrial census, geological surveys, etc.,★

spelling out a number of investment opportunities,

systematizing the most pressing economic and social needs,

making publicly known the government's *intentions* in the sphere of economic and social services, and

encouraging private investment (to the extent that previously mentioned aspects have bearing on private investment decisions).

All this is, of course, useful but still grossly inadequate. Properly speaking, the perspective plan is only a supplementary means for reaching proper current decisions, but is not itself a set of decisions. If not followed by a series of operative plans supported by an appropriate mechanism of their fulfilment, it is bound to remain on paper.†

Conclusion: Effective economic planning requires the construction of a planning mechanism consisting of a perspective plan, operative plans and the mechanism for their implementation. Perspective planning itself is a necessary, but only preliminary step in constructing such a planning mechanism.

Third observation: There is a functional relationship between the required rate of growth and the mechanism necessary to implement it. This relationship can be formulated as follows: the higher the rate of growth, the more centralized management of the national economy is required. In other words, the

---

★ Even this benefit is frequently short-lived, however, as in most cases this 'fact finding' campaign is organized on the *ad hoc*, rather than permanent basis, and economic data tends to become obsolete quite quickly. Moreover, because plan construction cannot take 10 years, the information gathered is usually very partial and subject to a great margin of error. In very few developing countries has the process of plan construction given rise to a permanent improvement of information flow, partly because in most cases the plan construction was not followed by the establishment of planning as a continuous process and of an appropriate planning mechanism.

† Usually the construction of a perspective plan has also a very limited impact on creating local planning skills, as the plan is drawn mainly by foreign experts, who depart after the planning document is ready.

higher the rate of growth, the bigger the role of physical planning and direct, specific government intervention and the smaller the role of general, monetary and fiscal policies.

It would be rather difficult to supply the full arguments behind this third observation, but if one accepts my notion of centralization (the use of administrative orders, physical allocation, and direct, specific government interventions as opposed to general, monetary and fiscal measures), then both historical experience and theoretical arguments seem to support my thesis.

When one thinks in terms of historical experience, the case of socialist countries and wartime planning of capitalist countries immediately springs to mind. In both cases the rapid acceleration of the growth rate with accompanying structural changes was achieved by centralized methods. I am also inclined to think that the sharp stepping up of the rate of growth can also be traced—significantly if not exclusively—to the recentralization which occurred in Poland two or three years after the changes introduced in 1956. The little I know of Japanese economic history—another celebrated case of rapid growth—seems also to support this observation. During the so-called Meiji Restoration the Japanese government was engaged on a significant scale in industrial ventures—only later on handing them over to private capital—and other *direct* measures.

Theoretical arguments seem to point in the same direction. The reasons why one cannot direct a war economy through the price mechanism also apply to a developmental policy aiming at rapid acceleration of the growth rate. The difficulties (including time lags) and the social and economic consequences of drastically increasing private savings and the channelling of them into socially desirable directions through the price mechanism are too well-known to deserve discussion here. Isolated examples of high growth rates and relative *laissez faire* (*e.g.*, West Germany) can quite easily be traced to a number of favourable circumstances (no military expenditures, huge influx of American economic aid, etc.) and as a rule refer to already developed countries. We have also to remember that economic development of industrial countries since 1850, spectacular as it is, appears very modest by recent standards, when expressed in terms of annual rate of growth. It amounted to 2·8 per cent. for total income and 1·8 per cent. for *per capita* income [3, p. 125]. But probably even the most determined critics of my third observation will agree that in developing countries there is a striking discrepancy between the high rate of growth postulated and the means envisaged to achieve it.

Conclusion: It is unrealistic to accept certain growth rates without at the same time accepting the policies necessary to achieve them. Unfortunately, this seems to be the fault of many developing countries. They postulate rates of growth which are very high in the light of previous achievements, and yet shy away from the drastic measures which would have been necessary for their implementation.

Fourth observation: Successful economic development requires not only drastic changes in the structure of production but also equally drastic changes in the structure of consumption. As a result, tools for inducing consumers to change existing consumption patterns are a necessary part of any effective developmental planning.

The disposable income of the population constitutes between 60 and 80 per cent. of gross national product (the latter figure being more appropriate for developing countries). In spite of this fact, the problems of moulding the consumption structure according to developmental requirements are usually only very partially taken into account in economic planning of underdeveloped countries.

Two problems have to be distinguished here:

First of all, there are the possibilities of substitution in consumption. Usually, measures in this direction hardly go beyond some effort at import substitution. But the problem is much broader than this. It is the problem of achieving the same consumption effect measured by consumption standards (*e.g.*, calorie intake, protein consumption, protection against climatic conditions, and the like) and consumers' satisfaction with minimum costs (or maximizing the consumption effects out of a given consumption fund). Consumption habits are usually both uneconomical (from the social as well as the individual point of view) and rigid, but when alternative means of satisfying a given need are provided and supported by proper inducement (*e.g.*, in form of lower prices) and promotional effort, substantial desirable changes in consumption patterns can be accomplished. These changes will then lead to higher consumption standards and/or less inputs for given consumption standards, measured both by consumers' satisfaction and appropriate consumption norms.*

The second problem is that in contrast to external economies in production, external economies in consumption are usually neglected in discussion of developmental policy. In spite of much talk about the need of changing social habits and values as a necessary part of successful developmental policy, the simple truth that the character of the society depends to a great extent on what it consumes is, as a rule, not properly taken into account in economic planning. In fact, however, successful economic development is impossible without 'cultural revolution'. Given a limited consumption fund, the cultural revolution requires substantial departures from market-determined price ratios of consumer goods and services in favour of consumption with high external economies (benefits). In the field of health and education this is usually taken into account in the form of free or subsidized services. In all but socialist countries, however, it rarely spreads into other spheres of consumption (*e.g.*, subsidized newsprint and books, cinema, radio and TV, passenger transport, basic foodstuffs, etc.) as it should. At the same time, keeping within the limit of a given consumption fund will necessitate heavy excise taxes (or turnover-tax) on other goods. Thus, the whole market structure of consumer goods prices has to be changed and adapted to the requirements of 'cultural revolution' and developmental needs.

Conclusion: Effective economic planning has to take fully into account the developmental potential of different consump-

---

* We may note that in contrast to producers consumers have much more limited knowledge of possible substitute means of satisfying their needs. Moreover, individual efforts in this direction cannot go beyond goods readily available on the market. Otherwise they are uneconomical, because they cannot benefit from economies of mass production.

tion structures, including external effects. This also means that policies for plan implementation cannot ignore the tools designed to bring about desired changes in existing consumption patterns.

2. *Socialist planning and developing countries*

To what extent can the techniques of planning and management used in socialist countries be of help in economic planning of developing countries ? First of all we have to realize that this is a much more narrow question than that referring to the socialist *methods of development*. The latter include the theory of social change as a necessary prerequisite for successful economic development and the theory of an effective *developmental path* to be followed for the sake of rapid economic growth. In this section, however, we shall be concerned only with relevance of socialist planning techniques to economic planning of developing countries.

Before we turn to brief examination of this problem, we have to define what we mean by developing countries, from the point of view of applicability and efficiency of planning.

The main differences in the planning mechanism, and consequently in efficiency of planning, between socialist countries and developing countries, are due to the fact that developing countries are so-called 'mixed' economies.

By a mixed economy I mean, in the *economic* sense, a multi-sectored economy, which consists of: (1) a public sector, (2) a subsistence sector (pre-capitalist sector), and (3) a capitalist sector which has (a) indigenous and (b) foreign components.

By a mixed economy I mean, in the *social* and *political* sense: (1) a compromise between different social forces, and as a consequence (2) 'the mixture of institutional motive forces' [7, p. 59] and 'government interventions . . . [which] are essentially pluralistic and are not organized into a monistic hierarchy of value' (ibid., p. 53).

In addition, by a developing country I mean, *organizationally* a country which has (1) a highly inadequate statistical and informational basis for planning and (2) a highly inadequate skilled-manpower base for planning.

If, for the sake of simplifying our discussion we disregard the social and political aspects of a mixed economy and assume throughout the presence of statistical and skilled manpower constraints, how does the multi-sectored character of mixed economies affect the relevance of socialist planning to problems of developing countries ? The following general observation can be offered.

The theory and methodology of perspective planning have the most *direct* relevance and applicability to the developing countries. This is due to the very character of perspective planning. The task of perspective planning is to work out a desired and feasible developmental path for the economy in the long run. Because the goals formulated in the perspective plan neither represent concrete tasks (they are not detailed enough to be a basis for immediate action) nor are addressed to any specific unit of national economy, the theory and methodology of perspective planning only very loosely depend on the institutional and organizational character of the economy in question. Due to this fact the theoretical, methodological, and practical experience of socialist countries accumulated in the course of constructing their long-term development plans is of direct relevance to developing countries, subject mainly to statistical and skilled manpower constraints. This is especially true in regard to planning the activities of the public sector in underdeveloped countries, which is in any case the major part of most of their plans.

In the field of operative planning and the tools of plan fulfil-ment the picture is much more varied and complicated. Here, both planning and the mechanism of its implementation are most intimately connected with the institutional and organiza-tional structure of the economy. I believe, however, that in this field, a number of conclusions useful for developing countries can also be drawn from experience of socialist countries:

Firstly, the experience of planning and management of socialist enterprises and industrial associations can be useful in directing the public sector in developing countries.

Secondly, some socialist countries (*e.g.*, Poland) have accumulated a wealth of experience in indirect planning and stimulating a private agricultural sector consisting of small peasant farms (which in Poland in 1962 still produced 88·7 per cent. of gross agricultural output).

Finally, in spite of vast institutional differences, there is also much to be learned from general methodology of operative plan building, including the significance of material balances and experience gained in the effort to apply input-output technique to national economic planning.

It is obvious, however, that due to the mixed character of their economy, developing countries need a number of tools of plan fulfilment specific to themselves. Some of these tools may show more resemblance to the tools of monetary and fiscal policies of industrial capitalist countries than to those of socialist countries. An extra word of caution is here required, however, which is now almost generally recognized by the profession, namely, that underdeveloped countries '. . . might be well advised to ignore most of the Keynesian apparatus . . .'. [[8], p. 110, and [4] p. 206–218, passim]

REFERENCES

[1] A. H. Hanson, *Public Enterprise and Economic Development*, London, 1960.
[2] B. Higgins, *Economic Development*, London, 1959.
[3] S. J. Patel, 'The Economic Distance between Nations: Its Origin, Measurement and Outlook', *Economic Journal*, March 1964.
[4] V. K. R. V. Rao, 'Investment, Income and the Multiplier in an Underdeveloped Economy', in Agarwala and Singh, *The Economics of Underdevelopment*, Bombay, 1961.
[5] I. Sachs, *Patterns of Public Sector in Underdeveloped Economies*, London, 1964.
[6] V. B. Singh, 'Need for Planning', *Co-existence*, May 1964.
[7] S. Tsuru, 'Merits and Demerits of the Mixed Economy in Economic Development', in I. Sachs, ed. *Planning and Economic Development*, Warsaw, 1964.
[8] L. Turgeon, 'Problems of Developing Countries', *Co-existence*, November 1964.
[9] F. J. Zimmerman, 'Are there Laws of Progress?' in *On Political Economy and Econometrics, Essays in Honor of Oskar Lange*, Warsaw, 1964.

PLANNING UNDER UNCERTAINTY: SOME PROBLEMS OF PLAN REVISION

Uncertainty as a result of imperfect knowledge

It is generally known that the actual performance of the economy never fully conforms to the planned targets and that quite frequently deviations are very significant indeed. The basic reason why these deviations occur can be summarized in two words: *imperfect knowledge.* Any action undertaken on the basis of imperfect knowledge is subject to *uncertainty* with regard to the final outcome. It is useful, however, to spell out the different aspects of imperfect knowledge, not only for guidance in our effort to improve this knowledge, but also for aid in devising a planning mechanism which can function with reasonable effectiveness under conditions of uncertainty.

It is, of course, difficult to offer a precise and satisfactory classification of the different aspects of imperfect knowledge, but the following may be of some help in indicating the basic problems which confront the planners.

First of all, there is uncertainty about the *data* which must be used in plan construction, and this is due to two kinds of imperfect knowledge: imperfect knowledge about the future and imperfect knowledge about the *present.* Obviously enough, human beings have very limited power to predict future events, and this is usually indicated as the major reason for uncertainty. But all planners have to act under conditions of imperfect knowledge about the *present* as well. The present is never fully known, and in developing countries knowledge of the present is especially meagre. The most basic data are frequently absent or subject to vast margins of error. Thus, 'the population of Nigeria', according to one expert opinion, 'is 45 million plus or minus 10 million'.

Both present and future causes of uncertainty can be mitigated, but the possibilities for improving our knowledge of the present are far greater than for the future. In developing countries, where partial knowledge of the present is a particular obstacle, great improvements are possible by organizing the proper statistical basis for planning.

The imperfect knowledge of planners about the basic data manifests itself in two ways in the planning process:

(1) In the form of wrong predictions: the values assigned to certain factors (e.g., international prices, increase of population) may turn out to be erroneous. Here we have a situation in which necessary factors were taken into account, but with wrongly estimated values;

(2) In the appearance of new factors which nobody predicted. Discovery of natural resources, inventions, wars, and natural disasters fall into this category. Though these factors do not appear in the plan directly, they need not be assigned zero values. In deciding the level of required reserves, certain provision for unexpected factors can be made.

The second important class of reasons for uncertainty comprises cases of imperfect knowledge about the *functional relationships* between different economic, technical, social and behavioural variables (as opposed to imperfect knowledge of the variables themselves). This leads to faulty assumptions. With the same body of information, *i.e.*, the same knowledge about the basic data, different plans will usually be produced by different teams of experts as a result of (1) differing evaluations of the basic data and (2) differing economic philosophies. The history of planning abounds with examples of faulty assumptions. Wrong estimations of marginal capital/output ratios may serve as a common technical example. Some other faulty assumptions are more intimately connected with the economic philosophies of the planners, such as that which stipulates that increased private profits = increased savings = increased capital formation, or, to take a contrary bias, that which stipulates that increased private profits = increased conspicuous consumption and/or unproductive investment = constant or diminishing capital formation.

Thirdly, imperfect knowledge can lead to faulty construction of the *mechanism for plan fulfilment*. In part this may reflect faulty assumptions. For instance, the belief that increase in private profits will increase capital formation can lead to a policy of inflationary credit expansion which may in fact increase consumption and/or unproductive investment. But in large part such faults in the mechanism for plan fulfilment may constitute an independent factor. For example, excise taxes intended to increase government revenue may be set so high as to actually diminish it. Policies designed to implement the plan may thus err by pushing it in the wrong direction or by not pushing it strongly enough. If one wanted to generalize, one might say that in socialist countries the main fault of tools of plan fulfilment is that some of them push in the wrong direction (the use of gross output as a success indicator for socialist enterprises is a classic example), whereas in developing countries the policies intended to implement the plan usually do not push strongly enough. The basis for criticizing the policies derives in both cases from their incompatibility with the targets of the plan.

Minimizing the dangers of uncertainty
Two courses of action are open to planners for coping with uncertainty. First, there is action aimed at reducing the level of uncertainty itself. Uncertainty due to imperfect knowledge about the present can be diminished by improving the sources of information on economic, demographic, technical and behavioural aspects of society. Improvement in statistics is the single most important step to be taken here. Uncertainty due to imperfect knowledge about the future can be lessened by influencing the course of some of the future events. Though this is usually beyond the control of planners of a single nation, it can sometimes be accomplished by agreement among a number of nations. Efforts to stabilize world prices of primary products have exactly this aim. Other devices for reducing future uncertainty are the co-ordination of long- and medium-term commercial agreements at fixed prices, which is also a common feature of trade between socialist states. Among

developing countries, the diminishing of uncertainty about the future is one of the major benefits that may accrue from closer economic co-operation.

Secondly, as uncertainty can only be diminished but never eliminated, the properly constructed planning mechanism must have certain built-in flexibilities and shock absorbers. Let us discuss these in turn.

The planning mechanism can derive its flexibility from the built-in relationship between the medium-term, say 5-year plan and the yearly operative plan. The rationale for formulating plan targets in the form of a medium-term plan is threefold. First, the time span is long enough for accomplishing most investment projects; secondly, during a 5 to 7 year period there is a fair chance that some random factors (*e.g.*, bad crops) will cancel out; and thirdly, there is time during the period for corrective action: since the basic weaknesses in the plan and the mechanism of its fulfilment usually reveal themselves during the first or second year, they can still be corrected within the planning period.

The basic shock absorbers are, obviously, reserves. The most important forms of reserves are in industrial capacities, inventories, and foreign exchange. The difficulty of maintaining a high level of reserves is due not only to the direct costs of the reserves themselves, but also to considerable reluctance to pay the indirect costs. Many socialist planners believe in the need for stimulating the economy with 'mobilizing tasks', tasks which require a maximum of productive effort. Without these, it is argued, there will be too much 'slack' in the economy and some potential increase in the growth rate will be sacrificed. There are, then, certain opportunity costs in failing to operate on the very frontier of production (as seen by the planners).

These costs, however, must be balanced against the benefits resulting from having extra reserves to cope with unforeseen events. It is the author's conviction, based on observation of Polish economic growth in post-war years, that the *realized* growth rate would actually have been higher and the developmental path smoother if bigger reserves had been available. This statement cannot, of course, be proved statistically, but the need for plan revision at the end of the Polish 6-year plan (1950–55) and again at the middle of the last 5-year plan (1961–65) clearly indicates that the 'shock absorbers' were inadequate, or in other words, that the planned rate of growth was too high. On purely analytical grounds, one can also argue that due to the interrelationships between different plan variables the failure to meet one of them leads to cumulative effects if proper reserves are not provided. It would be unfair, however, if we did not stress the practical difficulties in estimating the proper level of reserves for the national economy as a whole and the political difficulties of maintaining them.

The Need for Plan Revision

When does the need for formal plan revision arise? First of all, plan revision is necessary if, for whatever reasons, the course of economic development deviates 'too far' from the planned targets. By 'too far' we mean that these deviations cannot be corrected during the remaining plan period either by altering the content of the yearly operative plans which remain or by cushioning the effect of deviations with existing reserves. Secondly, the need for plan revision may arise due to the occurrence of new investment opportunities which are more productive than those provided for in the plan. The discovery of new natural resources or of important new inventions are cases in point. If taking advantage of these new investment opportunities requires forgoing some of the investments envisaged in the plan, revision of planned targets will be necessary.

When it becomes apparent that the originally formulated goals cannot be attained we are faced with the problem of re-grouping our economic forces and formulating new goal functions. This is not always easy to solve. Even in a simple case when we learn before beginning to implement the plan that 10 per cent. less foreign exchange will be forthcoming than was anticipated, we cannot simply contract our plan by 10 per cent. We must take account of (1) indivisibilities in production and (2) discontinuities of the goal function. The latter means that the planner's preference map is such that beyond a certain point the marginal rate of substitution between different planned goals, say education and defence, diminishes so rapidly that for all practical purposes no substitution is possible.

The most frequent case, however, is that some sectors develop according to planned targets while others lag behind. The need for plan revision is then imperative to prevent serious imbalances which may have political as well as economic consequences. The main cost of plan revision is that as a rule some investment projects must be frozen in their uncompleted form. To minimize this danger it has been proposed to adopt a time pattern of investment which will more evenly distribute the initiation of new investment over the entire planning period instead of concentrating it at the beginning. This will give the planners more flexibility, as the investment funds will not be fully committed from the very start. If this measure is coupled with 'rolling' 5-year planning—in which another year is added to the plan as each year is completed—it could smooth economic growth considerably. In present practice, the undertaking of new investments tends to be concentrated at the beginning of each medium-term plan, producing fluctuations in the growth rate and living standards.

Can there exist the situation when in spite of the fact that actual development deviates seriously from original plan, it may be unnecessary to revise the plan formally ? The question may seem strange at first glance, but it was actually posed and vigorously debated at the 1965 Annual Meeting of the Nigerian Economic Association, Ibadan.

The need for plan revision arises only when planning has some *binding* force, when there is the danger that certain sectors of the economy will pursue the original plan, which is no longer optimal in the new situation. If the plan is not really binding, that is, if actual practice has only a loose resemblance to the original blueprint, then it may be better to concentrate on creating preliminary conditions of effective planning for the future rather than wasting effort on revising the plan.*

* This seems to be the situation in Nigeria, if I have not misinterpreted Dr. O. Aboyade's arguments. See his paper 'Problems in Plan Revision', *Nigerian Journal of Economic and Social Studies*, June 1965.

Finally, it is worthwhile to stress that revision of the planned targets must always be accompanied by revision of the policy instruments. It is difficult to find a planning failure where faulty methods of implementation are not at least partially responsible.

A METHOD OF CONSTRUCTING
A PERSPECTIVE PLAN*

I

'As perspective planning deals to a considerable extent with the problem of choosing the appropriate growth rate of the national income it is necessary to say a few words about this concept as it is commonly used in the socialist countries. In contrast to its use in capitalist countries, it excludes the production of services. True, so-called "material services", such as transport, laundry, catering and even trade are included. However, the national income does not include the administrative services of the government, entertainment, education, medical services etc. Also excluded from the national income are services rendered by such fixed assets as residential houses, hotels etc.

'I believe that for the purpose of long-term planning this approach has something to commend it. It is easier to measure the real value of commodities than that of services. For instance, in statistics of capitalist countries the real increase in administrative activities is measured by an index of officials employed, weighted according to the salaries in the basic year. No account is taken—and hardly could be—of changes in productivity of labour in this case.

* What follows is a summary of two articles by Professor Michal Kalecki from the Central School of Planning and Statistics, Warsaw: (1) 'An Outline of a Method of Constructing a Perspective Plan' published in *Essays on Planning and Economic Development*, Warsaw, 1963 and (2) 'Plan perspektywiczny na lata 1961–1975' ('Perspective Plan for 1961–1975'), *Nowe Drogi*, August 1958. The growth equation is borrowed from another article by Professor Kalecki, namely (3) 'Zagadnien teorii dynamiki gospodarki socjalistycznej' ('On the Theory of Economic Dynamic of Socialist Economy') published in *Zagadnienia ekonomii politycznej socjalizmu* [*Problems of Political Economy of Socialism*], Warsaw, 1959.

'For other reasons, it is convenient not to include residential rent in the national income. The capital coefficient is very high in this case, and therefore the application of a general capital coefficient to the national income, in which residential rent is included, is fairly meaningless because such a coefficient is greatly influenced by the relative share of residential building in total investment.

'Our approach does not mean, of course, that services should be neglected in long-run planning. They are accounted for by appropriate planning of employment (for instance, in the case of the administrative activities of the Government) or by planning the capacities of consumer type fixed assets (*e.g.*, dwelling space).

'In line with the concept of national income used here we distinguish in planning between *productive* and *unproductive* investment (my italics—JGZ). By productive investment, 'we mean that destined for the production of goods and material services, while other investment, such as construction of dwelling houses, streets, parks etc. is classified as 'unproductive investment'.

'Before proceeding with the main subject of the paper, it is necessary to mention that in the Polish perspective plan *no accrual of foreign credits is assumed* (my italics—JGZ) and such also will be our assumption in the subsequent discussion. This approach does not differ substantially from one assuming an accrual of moderate foreign credits which are fixed beforehand in amount. On the other hand, the difference between our approach and the assumption that any gap in foreign trade, however large, will be always covered by credits, is of crucial importance; for such an assumption would completely eliminate the problem of balancing foreign trade which, as we shall see below, emerges as an essential factor in our approach to perspective planning.' (Kalecki [1], p. 9–10)*

2

The average annual growth rate of the national income may be considered the most important parameter of long-

* See footnote p. 135.

range planning. Usually, but not always, the government tends to develop the country as fast as possible. There will be, however, a number of limiting factors which must be considered. Two of them are especially important and relevant for underdeveloped countries:

(1) The higher the rate of growth, the higher the relative share of productive investment in the national income. This will unfavourably affect consumption and unproductive investment in the short run.

(2) Increase in the rate of growth creates difficulties in equilibrating the balance of payments. It is very likely that at some level of the rate of growth balancing foreign trade becomes impossible. Therefore there is an absolute limit to the rate of growth.

In some countries the scarcity of labour is also a limiting factor. It can be overcome by sufficiently increasing the capital outlays in the plan but this will again aggravate the problem of the relative share of investment in national income. In most underdeveloped countries, however, this factor is not present, at least for the range of the rates of growth of national income which come under consideration. Usually, their problem is the opposite one: how to create a sufficient number of new jobs for the existing labour force.

The first step in constructing a perspective plan is to make a crude outline of the plan assuming a rate of growth which is high in the light of the particular country's past experience (or failing this, by considering the experience of other countries in similar conditions). The second draft of the Polish perspective plan assumed the following average annual growth rates of national income: 1956/60—7·8 per cent., 1961/65—6·6 per cent. and for 1961/75—6·5 per cent. As Professor Kalecki points out, at the initial stage of preparation of a perspective plan we deliberately choose a high variant which it may be necessary to scale down even at the stage of preliminary testing. The quoted figures, however, are already subsequent to this testing stage.

The growth of national income may be considered as being determined by the following factors:

$$\frac{dGNP}{GNP} = \frac{I}{GNP} \times \frac{1}{k} + u - a$$

where:

    $dGNP$ = annual increment of GNP.

    I = annual gross productive investment outlays.

    k = capital-output ratio.

    u = technological and organizational progress factor tending to raise national income independently of the investment effort.

    a = capacity-reducing coefficient connected with the retirement of obsolete and worn-out plant and equipment.

Hence, the next steps in the construction of a perspective plan are some assumptions about the capital coefficient which relates the increment of national income to *productive* investment and some assumptions about the net results of 'u-a', which can then be translated into a higher (or lower) capital-output ratio. At this stage of planning, the assumed capital-output ratio is only a very crude approximation because the capital coefficient largely depends on the as yet undetailed *structure* of increment of output. The second draft of Polish perspective plan finally assumed the following capital-output ratios:

	1956/60	1961/65	1961/75
Productive investment in per cent. of nat. income Average annual increase of national income	$\dfrac{18\cdot8}{7\cdot8}=2\cdot4$	$\dfrac{20\cdot0}{6\cdot6}=3\cdot0$	$\dfrac{19\cdot3}{6\cdot5}=3\cdot0$

Assumed capital-output ratios seem rather low, but this is chiefly because only productive investment is included. In fact, higher capital-output ratios were assumed than during the period 1956–60. The quoted capital-output ratios were reached after careful examination of factors influencing the level of capital coefficient.

Among factors pushing it up we can list:

(1) structural changes in national economy: the expansion of branches with high capital-output ratios,

(2) more limited possibilities of increasing production from existing investment than was the case in the previous period; *e.g.*, when the number of shifts reaches 2·4–2·6 level, this means of better utilizing existing investment is already practically exhausted, and

(3) higher share of replacement investment in total investment.

Among factors diminishing the capital-output ratio, main stress was laid on diminishing the share of construction and installation works in the total value of investment. Their share is supposed to diminish from 60 per cent. in 1961–5 to 57 per cent. in 1961–75. The necessary share of productive investment is lessened by 0·6 per cent.

Now, having accepted some level of capital-output coefficient, we obtain the first approximation to the annual productive investment in the perspective plan, say, at its beginning, at its end, and in the middle. The figures assumed in the second draft of Polish perspective plan were: 18·8 per cent. for 1956–60, 20·0 per cent. for 1961–65 and 19·3 per cent. for 1961–75.* Then, we calculate, in a similar way, the necessary increase in inventories and by deducting it together with productive investment from the national income, we finally determine the sum of consumption and unproductive investment at the beginning, at the middle, and at the end of the perspective plan.

The next step in constructing the perspective plan is to split this last item into two components: consumption of goods and unproductive investment. The growth of unproductive investment is determined so as to achieve certain goals in housing, communal services, health services, education etc. These goals, in comparison with the present state of these services, determine the necessary level of unproductive investment.

'Already at this stage',—Professor Kalecki points out,—'we may find out that the relative share of productive investment plus the increase in inventories in the national income is so

---

* The *total* gross investments were accordingly assumed as 29·1 per cent., 31·6 per cent. and 31·5 per cent. of GNP.

high as to make the plan untenable because the inroads into consumption and unproductive investment would be too formidable in the short-run. However, since the result depends to a great extent on the level of capital coefficient which is altogether hypothetical in character—it may be safer even in such a case to pursue the variant somewhat further' (Kalecki [1], p. 13).*

3

Thus far we have split the national income into four components: productive investment, increase in inventories, unproductive investment, and consumption. If we then make some assumptions about the future structure of consumption, we may proceed to a crude determination of the industrial structure. As Professor Kalecki points out 'this is necessary for two reasons: for testing the balance of trade and for obtaining a second approximation to the capital coefficient which would reflect the structure of the increment in output' (Kalecki [1], p. 14).*

Table 1 presents the anticipated structure of consumption assumed in the second draft of the Polish perspective plan (Kalecki [2], p. 37):*

Table 7

Share in total consumption in %

	1960	1965	1975
Foods	48·5	45·0	38.0
Stimulants	9·2	7·7	5·1
Clothing and shoes	21.0	21·4	20·4
Durable consumers goods	8·2	10·7	11·8
Other goods	5·5	7·4	7·5
Non-material services	7·6	7·8	8·0
Non-specified goods	—	—	9·2
Total	100·0	100·0	100·0

In planning the consumption structure, a number of elements are taken into account: the structure of consumption

* See footnote p. 135.

in more developed countries, income elasticities of demand derived from family budgets, desired changes in consumption for economic, physiological or social reasons. In planning the consumption structure in our perspective plan, we encountered a number of problems, which may be of some interest:

1. The share of food consumption is diminishing, a normal phenomenon accompanying increase in the standard of living. In 1975 the level and structure of food consumption will be close to the optimum postulated by physiology. Its share of the total income will approximate that at present existing in richer Western European countries.

2. An especially drastic drop is anticipated in the consumption of stimulants, as a result of a hoped for reduction in alcohol and cigarette consumption. The absolute increase in the consumption of stimulants is 7 per cent., as compared to 50 per cent. increase in food consumption and more than 90 per cent. in total consumption.

3. The main increase in consumption is anticipated in consumer durables (190 per cent.). At the same time, however, the increase of passenger cars will be very modest: in 1975 we expect to reach the level of West Germany in 1958 per 1,000 population. This is, again, mainly due to balance of payments considerations. Import of crude oil and other petrol products will constitute in 1975 10 per cent. of total import—as much as import of wool and cotton together. As a result of all these considerations—together with the assumed long-term use of consumer durables—a loophole developed in our anticipated consumption structure, in the form of 'unspecified goods 9·2 per cent'. Although it is right not to specify all forms of consumption in such a long period, the percentage of 'unspecified goods' seems to be too high, and indicates the need of reworking this part of the perspective plan.

When we already know the desired volume and structure of consumption, in addition to our assumptions about the volume of productive and unproductive investments and increase in inventories, '. . . it is possible to make a rough estimate of the home demand for the products of the various branches of the economy. This involves, of course, some knowledge of the technical coefficients of production with allowance for the future technical progress and also some decisions as to the choice of technological variants . . .'. These decisions, however, have to be considered a first approximation only, to be changed later on in an effort to balance the plan.

Our rough estimate of the home demand for the products of the various branches of the economy must then be compared with the production possibilities of the economy in the period under consideration. Before we proceed any further we have to distinguish between supply-determined and demand-determined branches of economic activity. Professor Kalecki defines them as follows. 'By supply-determined industries we mean those activities which have a certain ceiling for the long-run rate of growth for technical and organizational reasons, so that even a considerable increase in capital outlay will not help to raise their output at a higher rate. The demand-determined industries have no such ceilings, at least for the range of the rates of growth of the national income which come into consideration. Thus the output of such industries can increase in the long run in accordance with demand' (Kalecki [1], p. 14).*

The technological and organizational factors which determine the ceilings of the rate of growth in supply-determined industries are varied. As examples we can mention: limited natural resources, the time necessary for adaptation of new technology, difficulties in recruiting manpower for certain industries (e.g., coal mining), the lack of adequate technical and managerial staff, long construction periods, etc.

In constructing the Polish perspective plan, a number of such ceilings were encountered. Let me mention some of them.

In the steel industry, to more than double the steel production within 5-years is considered technically and organizationally impossible.

In coal mining, the long period of construction (8–10 years) is the main obstacle. Every effort to increase coal production leads to an increase in the number of coal mines simultaneously

* See footnote p. 135.

under construction, and here again, there is only a limited number of coal mines that we can efficiently build at one time. Increasing this number only prolongs the average construction period and does not increase production.

In agriculture it was considered unrealistic to assume higher yields than 21 cetnars (1 cetnar = 100 kg) per hectare. (In 1962 actual yields were 16·1 cetnars.) One can argue that by increasing the amount of artificial fertilizers the yields could be further increased. But are the peasants ready for an increase in artificial fertilizers which is drastic in comparison with the present level?

After this digression, let us turn back to our 'rough estimate of the home demand for the products of the various branches of the economy'. First, we have to compare it with the production possibilities of supply-determined industries. This will enable us to ascertain how much of their product is left for export and how much it is necessary to import. 'Commodities which cannot be manufactured at home will also obviously be included in the import requirements. However, the determination of import requirements will have to allow for possible home produced substitutes for imported raw materials.

In this way, the first approximation of the total demand for imports will be reached. After deducting from their value those exports provided out of the surpluses of the supply-determined industries, one finds how much remains to be covered by the exports of demand-determined industries. Now, the production of these industries must be fixed in such a way that: (a) they fulfil the home demand for their products, (b) the total of their contributions to export cover the remaining part of import requirements mentioned above' (Kalecki [1], p. 16).*

Setting the production of demand-determined branches in the way just described ensures the balanced equilibrium of the plan, including balance of payment equilibrium. Unfortunately, equilibrium achieved in such a way may be of no practical significance, since it tacitly assumes that it is possible to place the exports in the foreign markets at the scale corresponding to the export plans required for such equilibrium. But this is

* See footnote p. 135.

6

frequently not the case. As Professor Kalecki points out: 'As a result of the pressure of the supply of the products in question their average prices may fall so low that it is impossible to obtain the revenue of foreign exchange required for purchasing the necessary imports. Or, even if this is possible, it may require capital outlays very high in relation to their effects in terms of foreign exchange, and as a result, it will aggravate the problem of the relative share of investment in the national income . . .' (ibid., p. 17).

In constructing our perspective plan, we had to take into account these limitations of foreign markets. Here are some illustrations:

(1) In order to equilibrate the balance of payments, our perspective plan assumed a drastic increase in machinery and equipment export and an equally drastic decrease in their import. The export of machinery and equipment has to increase from 21 per cent. in 1960 to 33 per cent. of the total export in 1975, while import must decrease from 19 to 8 per cent. It was considered unrealistic to assume higher figures, as *e.g.*, the share of machinery in German export in 1960, excluding passenger cars, was also $33\frac{1}{2}$ per cent.

(2) Food export ought to double in 15 years. This could be increased further but foreign markets are limited and price competition cannot go too far, as we have to import fodder to produce bacon, meat etc.

To summarize, the export plan cannot be a result of simply setting the volume of demand-determined industries at the appropriate level, but has to take into account the existing limitations of foreign markets. The whole plan has to be reconsidered in the light of these limitations. First of all, it may be possible to balance the plan by appropriate changes in methods of production. We do not assume constant technical coefficients. Some of the changes in technical coefficients have, let us say, 'automatic' character. For instance, substantial increase in new power plants automatically diminishes the amount of coal per 1 kWh of electric energy. Another, and probably most important, part of changes in technical coefficients results from conscious choices in methods of production, choices which aim at securing the balance equilibrium of the plan. For example, the electrification of railroads substantially diminishes the demand for coal, the development of chemical industry diminishes the demand for natural fibres, wood, steel etc.

If the feasible changes in methods of production are not sufficient to assure the balance of payments equilibrium, there is still the possibility of changing the structure of final demand so as to have lesser import content. For example, in the Polish perspective plan 1961–75, the level of unproductive investment was fixed relatively high. It must be noticed, however, that reduction of unproductive investment has little impact on balance of payments equilibrium, as they have relatively little 'import content'. As a result, reduction of unproductive investment can have little impact on increasing consumption of goods or productive investment—except some infrastructure investment such as roads—and the main result of cutting it down would be reduction in the growth rate of the national income. If, after all these changes, the balance of payments equilibrium still cannot be achieved, the rate of growth of national income will have to be *scaled down*.

Before we are ready to reconsider our initial assumptions about capital coefficient and necessary volume of productive investment, the balance of supply and demand for labour has to be considered. In planning employment in our perspective plan, several assumptions were made concerning both supply and demand for labour force.

On the supply side the following assumptions were made:

(1) The level of employment in agriculture throughout the 15-year period will be kept constant. The entire increase of population in agriculture will go to non-agricultural employment.

(2) The share of the gainfully employed in the total population will also remain constant. This second assumption was based on the fact that the proportion of women already in the labour force is *circa* 35 per cent., the level existing in most industrialized countries.

On the demand side, the following assumption was made:

The working week would be reduced from 48 to 40 hours, which is tantamount to a demand for an additional 650,000 persons.

On the basis of these assumptions on the one hand and demographic prognosis on the other, the balance of the labour force was then constructed.

When this is completed '. . . we can proceed with estimating again the total productive investment. This estimate may differ considerably from the first one made on the basis of a hypo-thetical capital coefficient. . . .We have then to reduce somewhat the rate of growth and examine the new variant in the way described above' (Kalecki [1], p. 19).*

* See footnote p. 135.

APPENDIX II

THE MECHANISM FOR MANAGE-
MENT OF SOCIALIST
INDUSTRY*

The Socialist Enterprise as a Cybernetic System. For the purpose of the theory of management it will be convenient to consider the socialist enterprise as a cybernetic system, consisting of:

(a) feeding system,
(b) information system,
(c) stimulation system, and
(d) steering system.

Graphically this is presented in diagram 5.

Feeding system

The enterprise is endowed with a given volume of fixed and variable capital. With the help of this capital the production process of the enterprise is being organized. The results of this production process—*goods* or *services*—are sold according to *buyer prices,* and a given total revenue is being realized. Before these receipts can again enter into the feeding system of the enterprise, they are subjected to two regulative processes:

* During the year and a half which elapsed after these lectures were written, the author's thinking on the problems of economic tools of plan fulfilment have undergone substantial changes. It would be impossible to present them fully here, but it is hoped that this appendix will give the readers some ideas as to the present approach the author uses in analysing this difficult and controversial subject. The study by the author on the mechanism for steering the socialist industry will appear (in Polish) in the not too distant future. This appendix was originally prepared for presentation to the International Seminar, organized by Centro Studi e Ricerche su Problemi Economico-Sociali, Milan, in Florence, September 14–16, 1966. It is reproduced here by kind permission of C.E.S.E.S.

Diagram 5

The Socialist Enterprise as a Cybernetic System: Simplified Diagram

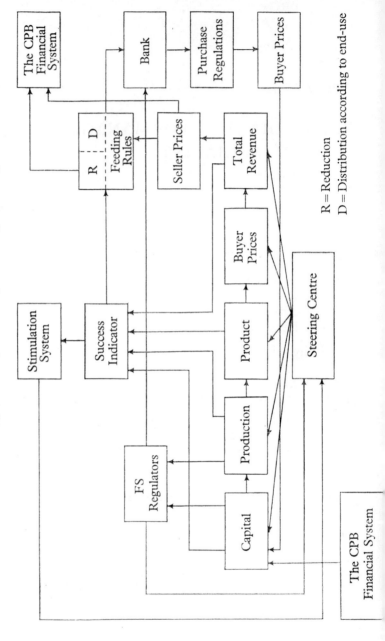

R = Reduction
D = Distribution according to end-use

(a) the first determines the total amount of financial resources which will remain at the enterprise's disposal;

(b) the second determines—to a certain extent—the use of the resources which remain within the enterprise. The circulation of this part of the total revenue which remains within the enterprise we call the *dependent* feeding system.

Because the socialist enterprise is a part of state ownership, we have to distinguish also the so-called *independent* feeding system. On the basis of macro-economic considerations the Central Planning Board (CFB) can decide that the resources of a given enterprise should be enlarged beyond the volume determined by the dependent feeding system. For example, it may be decided that the enterprise will be substantially expanded. Such steps are financed from the centralized investment fund and this flow of resources we label the independent feeding system.

Information system

The activity of the enterprise can be subdivided into a multiplicity of *economic events*: the employment of raw materials and manpower, the production of certain goods and services, etc. These economic events or certain of their features are registered according to existing *transformation rules* (methods of accounting) which determine what is to be registered and in what way. There are, for example, rules of registering the use of electric power, the employment of manpower, the volume of output, the level of costs, etc.

We shall call economic events or their features, aggregated according to transformation rules and usually compared to certain bases or norms, *analysers*. By analysers we understand all kinds of performance indicators pertaining to the whole or some part of the enterprise activity, *e.g.*, unit use of raw materials, level of costs, level of stock, quality of product, etc. As a rule, analysers are equipped with standards, bases of comparison, *e.g.*, input norms, planned level of unit costs, planned volume of output, profit, and the like.

In every enterprise there is a multiplicity of analysers serving different tasks. These tasks can be divided into general—being fulfilled by all analysers, and specific—by some of them.

The general task of all analysers is to 'watch' economic events and supply the enterprise steering centre (the management) with information necessary for operative decisions. The general character of this task reveals itself by the fact that all analysers are connected with the steering centre.

In addition to this general task, some groups of analysers aim at specific goals. We can subdivide them into three main groups:

(a) *Success indicators*, which are connected with the stimulation system. Within given limits they are the main determinants of enterprise strategy and tactics. Dozens of different success indicators have been used simultaneously or consecutively in socialist countries.

(b) *Regulators of the feeding system* (FS regulators). They are connected with the feeding system and regulate and control the flow of resources or of specific types of resources. The most important FS regulators are the so-called 'output indices' which are the basis of planning and controlling employment and the wages fund of enterprises and industrial associations.

(c) Technico-economic analysers which are the tools of control of specific processes within the enterprise, *e.g.*, use of inputs, quality of output, etc. They are connected with the steering centre by the information system only, and—sometimes —by the stimulation system with the lower echelons of managerial hierarchy.

We have to bear in mind that frequently the same analyser, let us say profit, fulfils more than one specific function. *E.g.*, profit is usually both success indicator and one of the FS regulators. We shall return to this problem later.

Stimulation system

One or several analysers are connected with the stimulation system of the enterprise. The construction of the stimulation system may vary greatly. The most simple stimulation system consists of three parts:

(a) success indicator (*MP*), which is, at the same time, the source of the bonus fund (*FP*),

(b) bonus coefficient (*W*), which determines the relationship between *MP* and *FP*, and

(c) the distribution coefficient (*P*), which determines how the bonus fund is to be divided between the members of the management. Consequently:

$$FP = MP \times W$$

and individual bonus (*FPi*):

$$FPi = MP \times W \times P.$$

In actual practice as experienced in socialist countries, the stimulation system is much more complicated and—as a rule—consists of the following factors:

(a) the rules for determining the volume of the bonus fund;

(b) the sources of its financing;

(c) the conditions which entitle the enterprise to establish the bonus fund (usually a certain level of success indicator has to be achieved);

(d) the conditions for paying the bonuses out of the bonus fund;

(e) rules of bonus fund distribution between members of the management.

The steering system

On an assumption of *ceteris paribus*, the steering system, *i.e.*, the strategy and tactics of the enterprise, is determined by the construction of the feeding, information, and stimulation systems. It means that the steering system can be meaningfully analysed only when the remaining systems are given. At the same time, the steering system can be used as a test of how effectively the other systems are constructed and functioning. If the behaviour of the enterprise does not conform to the CPB objectives, it means that there is a fault somewhere in one or several of the other systems. It is an important task of economic analysis to find out where in the remaining systems lie

the causes of the undesirable behaviour of the enterprise, and
to indicate the proper remedies.

The management mechanism

For an effective management of plan fulfilment the CPB needs
a properly constructed management mechanism. The management mechanism can be defined as a system of interrelated
tools of economic policy used for directing the economic activities of economic units, within the framework of the same form of
ownership.[1] The tasks of management mechanism consist of:

(a) inducing the economic units to plan fulfilment;

(b) inducing the economic units to economic behaviour
within the process of plan fulfilment and outside of it.

The elements of management mechanism

The management mechanism consists of three parts:

(a) The information transmitting system from and to the
CPB. In socialist countries there are four basic *information
carriers* presently in use:

1. prices,
2. plan indices: obligatory (administrative orders) and informational,
3. rates of bonuses, and
4. operational changes in the information and/or stimulation
   systems.

(b) The principles of the functioning of enterprises which
we shall call the *management formula*.

(c) The macro-economic feeding system which consists of the
financial-credit system and rules concerning the purchases of
inputs and of selling outputs. The management mechanism is
presented graphically in diagram 6.

Diagram 6 indicates that the enterprise is influenced by
transmitted information and/or by macro-feeding systems
through its management formula. This simple thesis is of
great practical importance, because it stresses the fact that the
manner in which the enterprise reacts to a given stimulus or con-
straint depends on how its management formula is constructed.

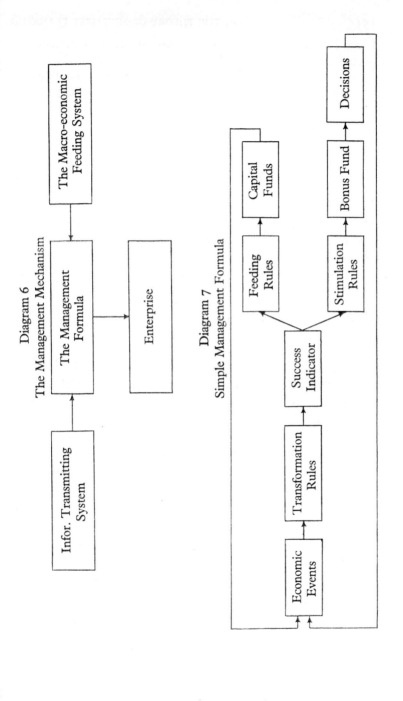

Diagram 6
The Management Mechanism

Diagram 7
Simple Management Formula

It can be generalized into the thesis of the integral character of management mechanism. The fact that all elements of management mechanism are closely interrelated within and between themselves is one of the basic causes of theoretical and practical difficulties of constructing efficient, internally consistent management mechanisms.

The management formula

Let us now consider in some detail the central part of the management mechanism—the management formula. Every management formula consists of the following elements:

(a) the methods of accounting, which transform certain features of economic events into success indicators and FS regulators;

(b) the success indicator or indicators and FS regulator or regulators;

(c) the stimulation rules (bonus regulations) which determine the interrelations between success indicators, bonus funds and management bonuses actually paid;

(d) the bonus fund or funds;

(e) feeding rules which determine the relationship between FS regulators and the enterprise capital funds (investment and operative);

(f) capital funds.

Depending on the construction of the second element of the management formula, we can distinguish here three basic types:

Type 1: A simple management formula, which consists of one success indicator which at the same time serves as the only FS regulator (see diagram 7).

Type 2: A complex management formula, which consists of one success indicator/FS regulator plus one extra FS regulator (see diagram 8).

Type 3: An exceedingly complex management formula in which the sum of success indicators/FS regulators is bigger than three (see diagram 9).

It is easy to supply actual and/or theoretical examples of all the three types of the management formula. Type one—

Diagram 8
Complex Management Formula

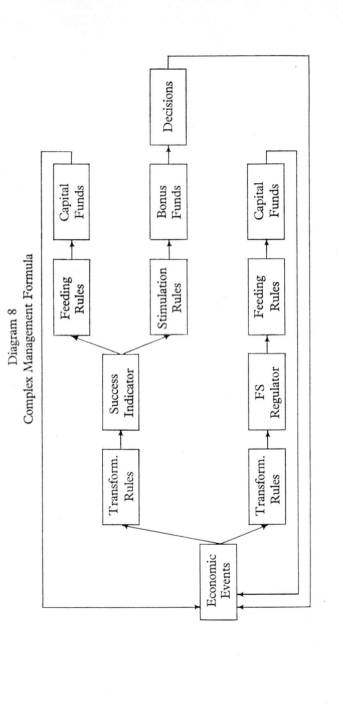

Diagram 9
Exceedingly Complex Management Formula

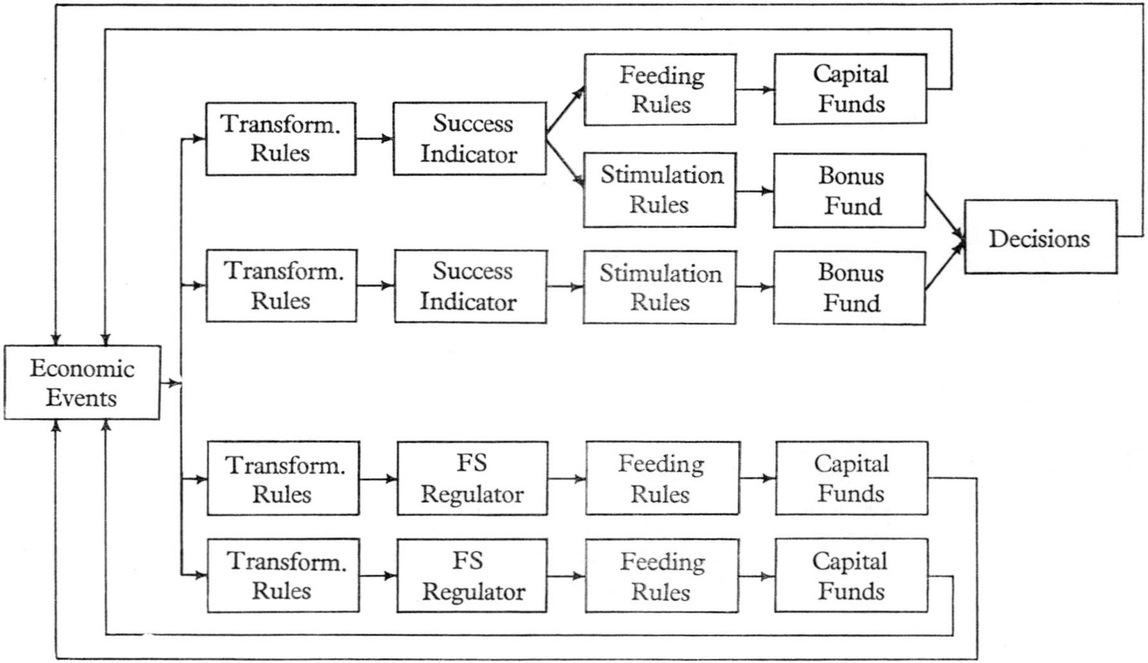

capitalist enterprise, Yugoslav practice and Czechoslovak proposed reforms; type two—some Polish proposals; type three —actual practice in Poland and in most socialist countries.

Different models for management of socialist industry

Depending on the type of the information carrier used by the CPB for managing the socialist industry, we can distinguish two management models:

(a) the parametric model, when prices and/or rates of bonuses are used;

(b) the non-parametric model, when administrative orders and/or changes in the management formula are used.

Model (a) uses *cipher* information, which must be deciphered by the information-stimulation systems of the enterprise. Model (b) uses *open* information.

Pure and mixed management models

Ex definitione, pure models are those where only one type of information is used: cipher or open. The actual practice of socialist countries represents a mixed model, in which both types of information are used simultaneously. This means that the management formula is constructed in such a way that it can receive cipher information. At the same time, however, open information is also used. Let us consider this problem in some detail.

The price information enters the enterprise management formula in the way depicted in diagram 10. Now, how does the open information enter the management formula? It would be false to visualize it as it is presented in diagram 11. We cannot ignore the fact that the actual management formula consists of the information and the stimulation systems which influence the reaction of the enterprise to open information. It is well known that, in practice, many administrative orders are not fulfilled, and this cannot be explained as being due to external circumstances only. On the contrary, to a great extent this is a result of a contradiction between the economic interests of the enterprise (determined by the construction of the information—stimulation

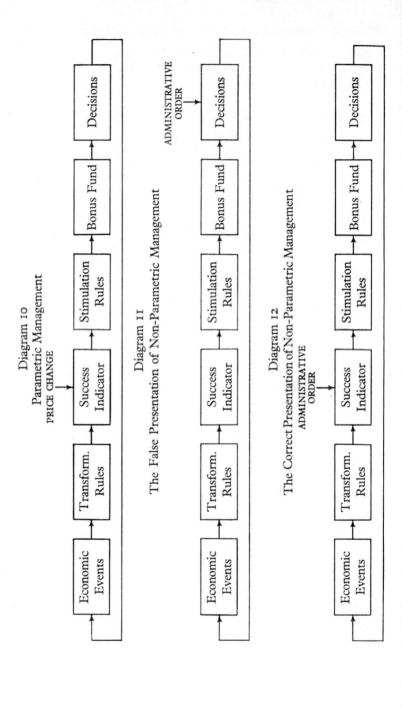

Diagram 10
Parametric Management
PRICE CHANGE

Diagram 11
The False Presentation of Non-Parametric Management

Diagram 12
The Correct Presentation of Non-Parametric Management
ADMINISTRATIVE ORDER

systems, and the cipher information entering them) and open information. The actual path of open information is presented in diagram 12. It means that the actual behaviour of the enterprise is a compromise between the actions dictated by cipher information and open information. There is ample evidence to support this thesis.[2] Needless to say, such a compromise would be unnecessary if both types of information contained exactly the same information. However, as we shall explain later on, for technical reasons, this is impossible.

Operational prices are used in management models
As we have indicated elsewhere[3] there are four types of prices used in present day socialist countries:

(a) programming prices, used for the construction of internally consistent plans; these prices are used for aggregation only and prevail in most of the actual planning exercises;

(b) shadow or accounting prices which are used for partial optimization in the process of plan construction; thus far these prices are used in investment and foreign trade effectiveness calculations only;

(c) operational prices used in the process of plan fulfilment, as one of the information carriers used in managing the socialist industry, and

(d) consumer goods prices which are, in principle, market-clearing prices for consumer goods.

Whenever we speak about prices in this paper we mean operational prices.

The construction of the management formula and the possibility of parametric management. The possibility of using cipher information depends—to a great extent—on the construction of the management formula, and especially on its information system.

The reception sphere of success indicators.
Every success indicator has a certain reception sphere. By the reception sphere of a success indicator we understand how many and what features of economic events are registered in a

success indicator, influence its magnitude. Needless to say, the range of the reception sphere of different success indicators shows marked differences.

We can use the range of the reception sphere as a criterion for dividing all success indicators into two groups:

(a) Success indicators with the broadest reception sphere we shall call *synthetic* success indicators. The broadest reception spheres have those success indicators which are *reducing* costs and revenues. Only success indicators based on profit are such *reducers*.

(b) All other success indicators we shall call *specialized* success indicators. Their characteristic feature is that their reception sphere registers economic events from the input *or* output side, never from both. No specialized success indicator is a cost-revenue reductor *ex definitione*.

The features of economic events are determined by:

(a) the activity of the enterprise itself; *e.g.*, diminishing the steel input per unit of output;

(b) information transmitted from the CPB; *e.g.*, price increase of steel will change the cost effect of a given steel input;

(c) information sent from the customers; *e.g.*, lack of orders may force the enterprise to change its product mix.

The success indicator can be considered as a receiver-transmitter, which receives different informations and transmits them to the enterprise steering centre and the CPB. This is presented in diagram 13.

The proper construction of the enterprise information system requires that the sensitivity of the proposed (or actual) success indicator to these three sources of information be carefully analysed. This is the problem of how broad or narrow is the reception sphere of a given success indicator. Another important problem in constructing the information system of the enterprise is to ensure the *proper reaction* of a success indicator to economic events. The change in economic events, which is considered as desirable by the CPB, should induce desirable changes—from the enterprise point of view—in the success indicator.

Table 8

Determinants of Reception Sphere and of
Type of Reaction of Value Success Indicators

Determinants	Construction of Success Indicator	Transformation Rules	Completeness of Price System	Principles of Price Fixing
Sensitivity to the activity of the enterprise itself	X		X	X
Sensitivity to the information transmitted from the CPB	X	X		X
Sensitivity to the information transmitted by customers	X		X	
Type of reaction to economic events and/or external information	X	X		X

For the sake of brevity we present the determinants of the reception sphere and the type of reaction of a success indicator in the form of a table (see table 8) without presenting proofs and illustrations.

The reception sphere and the parametric management.

For the purpose of management theory it is useful to distinguish the following concepts:

(a) the sphere of enterprise activity (activity sphere), which covers all economic events within the enterprise;

(b) the sphere of enterprise authority (authority sphere), which covers those economic events over which the enterprise has the power or the right to command;

(c) the reception sphere of success indicators, which—as already defined—cover those economic events which are registered in success indicators.

Diagram 13

The Success Indicator as a Receiver-Transmitter

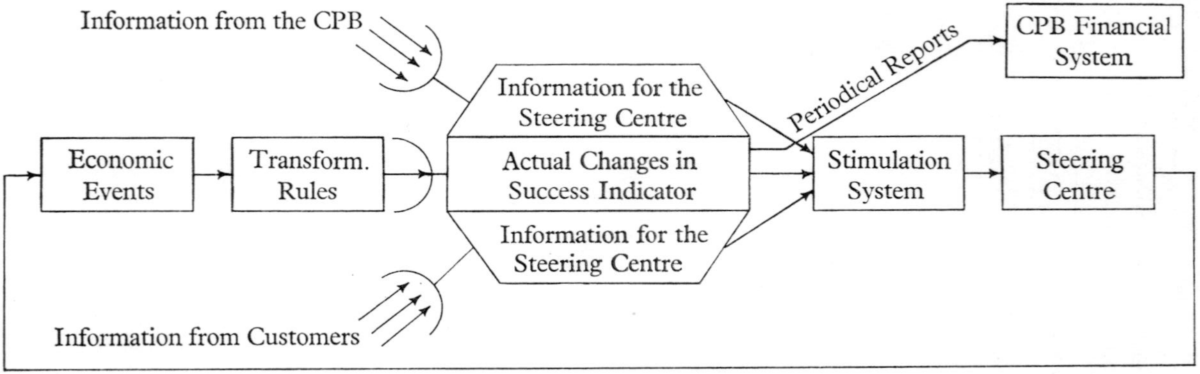

Information from the CPB

Information for the Steering Centre

Actual Changes in Success Indicator

Information for the Steering Centre

Economic Events

Transform. Rules

Information from Customers

Periodical Reports

CPB Financial System

Stimulation System

Steering Centre

Diagram 14

The Reception Sphere and Parametric Management

Activity Sphere = Reception Sphere

| Authority Sphere | The Sphere of CBP Decisions |
| The Sphere Governed by Cipher Information | The Sphere Governed by Open Information |

In all multi-level economic structures—from capitalist business corporations to socialist industrial associations—the activity sphere is broader than the authority sphere. This part of the enterprise activity—activity sphere minus authority sphere—must be, *ex definitione*, governed by open information. The use of parametric management cannot go beyond the range of the reception sphere and the authority sphere. In properly constructed management formulae, the reception sphere is equal to the activity sphere and the parametric management is confined to the authority sphere. This leads us to an obvious thesis that the necessary prerequisites for wider use of prices require:

(a) a broadening of the reception sphere of success indicator/s,
(b) a broadening of the sphere of the enterprise authority.

The above relationships are presented in diagram 14. In actual practice we frequently encounter the violations of these relationships. The reception sphere of success indicators is often narrower than the authority sphere, which leaves out—for the time being—some activities which are not steered by the CPB. This leads to efforts to broaden the reception sphere or—if these are unsuccessful—to extend the sphere of open information and—as a result—to diminish the authority sphere.

Changes in management formula as a steering device

Thus far we have discussed the situation where the management formula is given and constant, and the CPB influences the behaviour of the enterprise by changing prices and/or administrative orders. However, in actual practice of socialist countries, changes in the management formula are frequently used as a semi-operational steering device. These changes in management formula usually occur in the information and/or stimulation system.

Changes in the information system as a semi-operational steering device

The introduction of new success indicators was a frequently used device for influencing the behaviour of the enterprise. It was a result of two phenomena.

First of all, the basic success indicator used—gross value of output—had a very narrow reception sphere. It resulted, as is well known, in very uneconomical behaviour on the part of the enterprise management. By introducing new, specialized success indicators—quality, cost reduction and the like—the CPB wanted to influence the enterprise behaviour in a desirable way.

The second reason was the policy of practically constant operational prices. With constant prices, the CPB was left with the remaining four types of information carriers: administrative orders, rates of bonuses, bonus conditions, and new success indicators. The last was used rather indiscriminately, and as a result, in 1960, approximately fifty success indicators were being used in the Polish industry.

The use of success indicators as a semi-operational steering device has a number of disadvantages. First of all it leads to their inflation. It is relatively easy to introduce new success indicators, but it is very difficult to eliminate success indicators once introduced. Every success indicator is a source of income to a certain managerial group, and the resistance to any effort to eliminate it is very powerful indeed, as the Polish experience has clearly shown.[4] From the management theory point of view, the use of narrow specialized success indicators means also that it becomes impossible to create the system of specialized success indicators which covers the whole activity sphere of the enterprise. It can be achieved with the help of two broad specialized success indicators: costs and output. The moment, however, we enter the path of narrow specialized success indicators, the task becomes impossible: there are hundreds of economic events within the sphere of activity of any enterprise.

Secondly, the use of specialized success indicators creates an exceedingly complex information system within the enterprise, with half a dozen or even a dozen different success indicators, each having a different reception sphere, specific transformation rules, a bonus system, etc. With such a complex information-stimulation system, the prediction of the actual behaviour of an enterprise becomes practically impossible.

A good example of a variable information system is the actual solution (introduced in 1964) of information—stimulation

Diagram 15

An Example of a Variable Information System
Poland, 1964 on

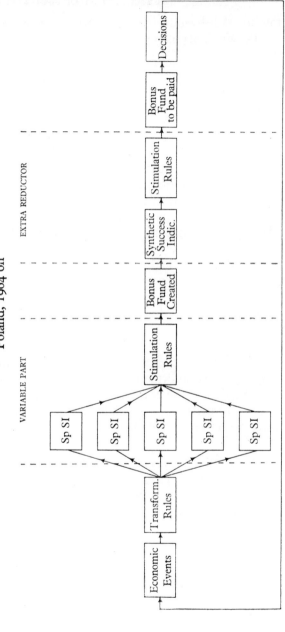

Sp SI = Specialized success indicator

systems in Polish industrial enterprises. It is depicted in diagram 15. We shall postpone our comments on it until the next paragraph.

Changes in stimulation system as a semi-operational steering device
The bonus system functioning in Poland in 1960–63 can serve as an illustration of a flexible stimulation system used as a semi-operational steering device. It is presented in diagram 16.

In both systems (diagrams 15 and 16), the industrial associations are given the right to change specialized success indicators or bonus conditions every year, as a tool for influencing the economic behaviour of the enterprises. In both systems, a synthetic success indicator acts as a necessary but not sufficient condition for obtaining bonuses. If a certain level of profit is not achieved, no bonuses are paid out to management; but even high profits do not entitle the management of the enterprise to a bonus, if certain specialized tasks have not been fulfilled.

The simultaneous use of different information carriers for transmitting the same information and the reliability of the management mechanism
The actual economic policy of socialist countries uses simultaneously different information carriers for transmitting the same information to the enterprise. For example, presently in Poland the information on desirable product mix is sent to the enterprise with the simultaneous help of three information carriers:

(1) administrative orders about required assortment;
(2) price ratio for different products;
(3) bonus ratio for assortment and other specialized tasks.

Today it is technically impossible to assure that these different carriers transmit exactly the same information. As a result, the product mix as determined by administrative orders differs from the product mix which would result from a profit maximizing behaviour with given prices, and differs also from the relative bonus attractiveness of fulfilling the assortment plan, rather than, let us say, introducing new products for which a

Diagram 16

An Example of Variable Stimulation System
Poland, 1960–63

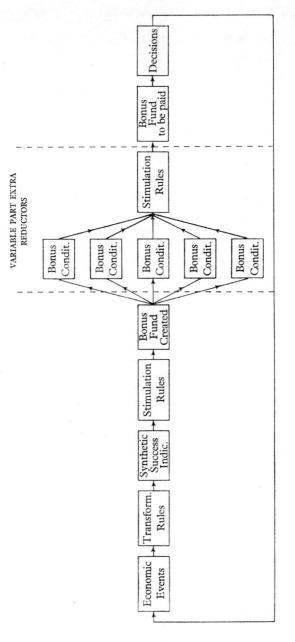

certain bonus value is also assigned. In this situation, by using different information carriers for transmitting the same information, we do not increase the reliability of management mechanism. Rather we diminish the effectiveness of each type of information.

The situation would be different if we used additional information carriers, whenever the existing one does not work. For example, with the linear horizontal cost function, the price of output does not constitute sufficient information to determine the proper volume of output. In such a case open information from the CPB would be valuable. But this open information is not repeating the same information which is already transmitted by the price system: it supplies additional information. The reliability of the system can be increased when there are additional information carriers ready for use when functioning information carriers do not work. As long, however, as they do function properly, additional information carriers should have zero value.

Concluding remarks

Both practical experience and theoretical considerations lead one to the conclusion that the way to improve the functioning of socialist economies lies in the direction of using success indicators with the broadest possible reception sphere (synthetic success indicators), strictly limiting the use of open information and using prices as the main information carrier. Such a system, however, requires that a number of conditions must be fulfilled—most of them not easy to achieve—for its proper functioning. Thus far—it seems—economists have been more successful in criticizing the non-parametric system than in drawing feasible blueprints—including the problems of transition—of the parametric one. The present author is no exception to this rule.

Notes

My thinking along the lines as set out in the preceding pages was greatly influenced by the works of O. Lange (*Introduction to Economic Cybernetics*), and particularly by Wieckowski's *Role of Profit in the Management of Production*, Warsaw, 1965.

The help and guidance thus received is gratefully acknowledged.

[1] Households and private farmers are influenced by the CPB with the help of the steering mechanism. The main difference between management and steering mechanisms lies in the fact that the latter consists of two elements only: information transmitting system and macro-economic feeding system. The principles of household or private farmers functioning are not determined by the CPB but by the nature of the economic unit involved.

[2] The Polish Minister of Internal Trade, Dr. M. Lesz, recently has also quoted a number of examples of not fulfilling the assortment plan and commented: [3] 'We have here a certain regularity, a certain law: the level of plan fulfilment of a given good is directly proportional to the value of production per hour of labour.' He traced it to the use of gross value of output as a main success indicator.

[3] The problem of prices is more fully discussed in [4], [5] and [7].

[4] The introduction of a new bonus system in Poland in 1960 (it was terminated in 1963) was accompanied by efforts to eliminate specialized success indicators and bonuses belonging to them. Only two specialized success indicators —out of over 50—were actually eliminated, however, because of the managers' resistance. [1, p. 119]

REFERENCES

[1] Bronislaw Fick, *Bodzce ekonomiczne w przemysle* (*Economic Incentives in Industry*), Warsaw, 1965.
[2] O. Lange, *Wstep do cybernetyki ekonomicznej* (*Introduction to Economic Cybernetics*), Warsaw, 1965.
[3] M. Lesz, *Bodzce i mierniki przedsiebiorstwa przemyslowego a potrzeby rynku* (*Incentives and Success Indicators of Industrial Enterprise and Requirements of the Market*).
Konferencja o miernikach oceny dzialalnosci przedsiebiorstwa. Materialy przedkonferencyjne (*Materials for Conference on Success Indicators*). In mimeographed form n.d.

[4] *Studies on the Theory of Reproduction and Prices*, Warsaw, 1964.
[5] A. Wakar and J. G. Zielinski, 'Socialist Operational Price Systems', *American Economic Review*, March 1963, 1, pp. 109–127.
[6] J. Wieckowski, *Rola zysku w kierowaniu produkcja* (*The Role of Profit in Production Management*), Warsaw, 1965.
[7] J. G. Zielinski, 'The Consumption Model and the Tools of Its Implementation', in *On Political Economy and Econometrics. Essays in Honour of Prof. O. Lange*, Warsaw, 1964.

17-32